William's book

FISHING

BLITZ

Author: Brian Furzer

Adviser: Brian Harris

Editor: Frances Ferneyhough

Cover design: John Strange

This edition published in 1991 by Blitz Editions,
an imprint of Bookmart Limited, Registered Number 2372865.
Trading as Bookmart Limited, Desford Road, Enderby,
Leicester LE5 5AD

Originally published in 1983 by Grisewood & Dempsey Ltd.

© Grisewood & Dempsey Ltd 1983.

ISBN 1 85605 052 1

Printed and bound in Italy.

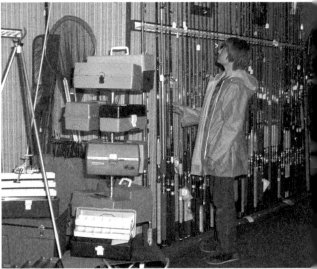

Contents

Going Fishing	8	Into the Net	73
Coarse Fishing	10	Where to Go?	76
Types of Fish	12	Choosing your Method	78
Rods, Reels and Lines	24	Dry Fly Fishing	80
Hooks, Floats and Nets	28	Wet Fly Fishing	82
Choosing Bait	30	Nymphing	84
What to Wear	34	Still Waters	86
Assembling Tackle	36	Coarse Fishing with Flies	89
Putting it Together	38	Sea Fishing	90
Where to Go?	40	Types of Fish	92
Float Fishing	44	Sea Tackle	96
Legering	46	Sea Bait	98
Spinning	48	Harbours and Piers	100
Casting	50	Casting	102
Playing and Landing	52	On the Rocks	104
Fly Fishing	54	Fishing Matches	106
Trout and Salmon	56	Safety and Conservation	108
Tackle for Trout	64	Where to Fish	110
Reels, Hooks and Knots	66	Books to Read, Societies to Join	111
Flies and How to Tie Them	68	Glossary	112
Casting a Fly	70	Index	114

Coarse fishing among the lily pads. These are a favourite with anglers, as they provide fish such as tench, carp, roach and rudd with shade and food. These fish in turn may attract predators such as pike.

Going Fishing

Many people think of fishing as simply sitting by the side of a river and watching a float upon the water, in any weather conditions. The simple truth is that fishing is what you make of it, just like everything else in life! You may be content to walk just a short distance and sit by a piece of river, within sight and sound of a busy road, and hope that some fish will oblige you by biting. If you are a little more adventurous and would like to catch bigger fish, you may try to tempt some of the fine fish that are in many, many waters throughout the British Isles. It is possible that you may be a very competitive type of person, and you would like not only to catch fish but to catch more than others; match fishing would appeal to you. It all depends on your time and energy, because there is good fishing almost everywhere in Britain.

Small but good
A fish does not have to be large to give you a lot of pleasure. I have caught many fish that could not ever

Fishing has a number of rules and regulations; we list the most important on page 110. They are all designed to protect fishing, so it is really important to keep them.

be regarded as specimens but which came from a difficult position, or were caught under very difficult circumstances. It gives me pleasure to accomplish the feat of beating the fish, not only by getting it to take the bait but also by presenting the bait or fly in a place that is difficult to fish. Such places are not on the map very often and you happen upon them by accident, but it is always fun exploring.

Types of fishing

There are three main types of fishing – coarse fishing, which covers most freshwater fishing except for salmon and trout; fly fishing, in which a fly (usually artificial) is used as bait to catch trout and salmon and occasionally other fish; and sea fishing.

In the following sections on coarse, fly and sea fishing, only the basic principles have been presented. There is far more to fishing, but it is only by fishing regularly and often that you will become expert at your chosen branch of fishing. It always helps too to look at what is going on in and on the water, because that sometimes gives you very good ideas on how to fish.

I hope the following information will be of help or inspiration to you, but do seek advice if you are in any doubt. Fishing can be very miserable if you are not catching anything and the weather is bad, and sometimes only a small change in tactics will make all the difference between success and failure.

Above: Casting from a beach – a more active way of fishing. No licence is needed to fish in the sea, and there is no close season.

Success – this young angler has caught two fine rainbow trout on the still water behind him. Trout fishing, once the pastime of rich and dedicated fishermen, is now something everyone can afford since reservoirs, lakes and pools are commonly stocked with fish.

9

Fishing is not just a summer sport; here an angler, well wrapped up against the cold, is fishing for chub under the willows of the river Windrush.

This splendid pike was caught on a Fenland canal. Pike are widespread in Britain, and are often the only coarse fish found in cold and fast-flowing trout streams. They are predators, feeding on other fish, and will sometimes attack the fish in your keep net! They are strong fighters and can provide very good sport.

Coarse Fishing

'Coarse' fish include all freshwater fish except salmon or trout. Dictionaries define the term coarse as meaning common or inferior, but there is really no good reason for describing the fish, or the fishing of them, in such terms. Whatever form of fishing is carried out, there are many skills involved and much pleasure to be gained.

Coarse fishing is carried on in inland waters such as lakes, rivers, canals and gravel pits, and there are many different methods to learn and many different species of fish which may be caught. Some fish feed only in certain areas of the water, such as at the bottom of the river or lake, and some fish will respond only to certain methods or baits. The most appealing thing about coarse fishing is that there are usually some coarse fishing waters available to everybody within easy travelling distance.

The simplest way of fishing is simply to dangle a bait on a hook into the water on the end of a line. But different methods have been developed to suit all different conditions of water and all types of fish. Most fishing is done with a rod, while floats and weights allow the bait to dangle in the water at a chosen depth or to lie on the bottom. The bait can be left in the water, or it can be drawn through it to attract the fish. As you gain experience, you will find out which sort of fishing you like best, and learn more and more skills.

Local conditions

The type of fishing which you will be doing, and the fish that you will catch, depend largely on the area in which you live. The tackle which you will need should be carefully chosen with local conditions in mind. Some shops, although not fishing tackle shops, have a department which will sell you fishing tackle. This is all very well if you have adult advice on what to buy, but if you have not, any fishing tackle dealer will be glad to offer you proper advice and help. This will be valuable because he knows the area and is always talking about fishing to the people who fish regularly in the waters around. The fact is that all anglers are willing to help a keen young beginner, so you can learn much if you are willing to listen and are not afraid to ask for advice or help.

Returning a huge 30-pound pike to the water. Most fish are returned as soon as possible after they have been caught. Make sure your hands are wet before handling them.

Unhooking a chub in the landing net. The less you handle fish the better, since this removes the protective slime with which their bodies are covered and damages their scales.

Types of Fish

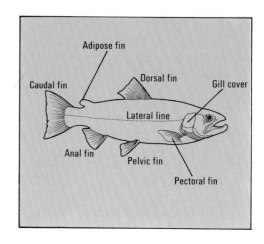

The main parts of a fish. The lateral line is a line of cells which are sensitive to vibrations and movement in the water.

The types of fish that are in your particular area depend absolutely on the waters available. Eels for instance can be found anywhere, as can roach, pike, perch and tench. But you will be very lucky if you live near to a good barbel river. The following fish are those most commonly caught in Britain.

Roach Every angler will catch a roach at some stage or another, whether he fishes in rivers, lakes or pits, whatever bait he uses and whatever way he fishes. It is an attractive silver fish with large scales and red fins. It will shoal in great numbers when it is small, but the big roach are not found in such large shoals. A roach is considered to be getting big when it weighs more than 1 pound (0·45 kg) and a specimen (as anglers call a better than average fish) is over 2 pounds (0·9 kg).

This fine roach was taken at night in a gravel pit; you can see how clear the water is. The roach's silver scales and bright red fins make it a particularly attractive fish.

Perch The perch is probably the most attractive fish

The colourful roach; a fish over 1 pound is considered quite large.

This perch, weighing 2½ pounds, is a really good fish. Large perch are very difficult to catch. They need careful handling because of their sharp spines.

that swims in British waters. Like the roach it shoals in large numbers when small, but becomes more solitary when it reaches greater sizes. A good perch weighs over 2 pounds (0·9 kg) and becomes a real specimen when it is more than 3 pounds (1·4 kg) in weight. It is a handsome fish with a strong, humped appearance and a large dorsal fin that is spiked and fearsome looking when erect. The perch must be handled carefully because the spines on the dorsal fin and gill covers can give you a painful wound. The back of the perch is olive-green in colour with darker stripes. It is a predatory (hunting) fish which will take other small fish, alive or dead, but will also take maggots and worms. Small perch are very greedy, while the large fish are cautious and not easily caught. The perch is a hard fighter and will test anybody's skills on light tackle.

Pike If any fish is a law to itself, it must be the pike, which abounds in rivers, streams, lakes and pits. Sometimes it will feed greedily but on other occasions it will not look at a bait which is dangled on its nose. It grows to a large size, and in the most

The perch is easy to tell by its spiked dorsal fin.

surprising places. Most small waters have stories of a huge, uncatchable pike which is forever breaking lines when hooked, but in truth the cause of breakage is usually clumsy angling!

The pike is shaped like a torpedo with its dorsal fin set well back along its body and with large pectoral and pelvic fins which make it very fast. It is green or yellowish green in colour, with broken stripes of a lighter colour which help to camouflage it. It is a predatory fish which lies among weeds, waiting until its prey swims close enough to be seized by virtue of the speed and grip of its toothed jaws. When you catch a pike, treat it with the greatest respect because its jaws are filled with large teeth and it has a very strong grip. Use pliers or forceps to remove hooks.

The pike can be caught on spinners, live bait and deadbaits, but it will sometimes take worms and maggots and even bread. A good pike weighs over 10 pounds (4.5 kg) and the magic weight everyone likes to achieve is 20 pounds (9 kg); all serious pike anglers dream of catching a 30-pounder (13.5 kg). Very, very few pike of more than 40 pounds (18 kg) have been caught in British waters.

This fine pike weighs over 24 pounds and is a catch to be proud of. Pike are great fighters, sometimes leaping right out of the water in their efforts to shake the hook loose. Be very careful when you remove the hook yourself; the pike's sharp teeth can give you a savage bite.

14

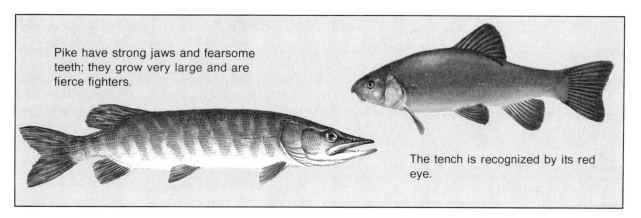

Pike have strong jaws and fearsome teeth; they grow very large and are fierce fighters.

The tench is recognized by its red eye.

Tench is the fish that everyone associates with summer. It can be caught mainly in still water but is often caught in slow-moving rivers. It is seldom found in swift-flowing water. It is not true, as some people suggest, that the tench buries itself in the winter, although it is certainly not often caught at that time of year.

The tench has a very large tail fin and the other fins with which it swims are also large. It is a really powerful fighter. The tench is usually a bottom feeder, and the common baits used for it are bread, worms and maggots although, like all other fish, it sometimes breaks the rules and will feed on unusual items. It is olive-green in colour with a red eye, by

The tench is easy to recognize by its olive-green to black colour, and its brilliant red eye. It is rare to catch a tench weighing less than a pound (0.45 kg), probably because very small fish feed in weed beds.

Tench is a summer fish, which gives much pleasure to anglers. It travels in shoals and is a strong fighter. This tench is being carefully returned to fight another day.

15

which it is known. A tench of more than 6 pounds (2·7 kg) is a specimen but the fish which shoal in sometimes large numbers are usually 2 to 3 pounds (0·9 to 1·35 kg).

Chub The chub is a blunt-headed fish with a large mouth, not particularly attractive but definitely a fish worth catching. It is common in all rivers and recently has become common in some still waters. It is a shoal fish when small and will feed anywhere in the water, from the bottom up to the surface. Large chub become solitary and live in places such as tree roots and beneath overhanging branches which are hard to get at. They feed on virtually anything from maggots and bread to crayfish. The most successful method used to catch large chub is a freelined bait, and floating crust can have really breathtaking results. A reasonable chub weighs 3 pounds (1.35 kg) and over with a specimen weighing more than 5 pounds (2·25 kg).

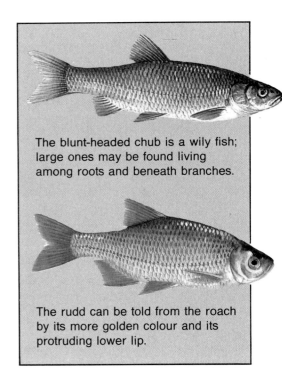

The blunt-headed chub is a wily fish; large ones may be found living among roots and beneath branches.

The rudd can be told from the roach by its more golden colour and its protruding lower lip.

A chub from the river Welland. The chub feeds on almost anything and often lives in very difficult places; specimen chub are hard to catch.

Rudd are beautiful fish, which in later life take on a golden colour and have red fins. The small rudd are often mistaken for roach although they are not as widespread. Because the rudd often feeds at the surface, its lower lip comes farther forward than the upper, whereas in the roach the upper lip protrudes. This is the easy way to tell the difference between rudd and roach, but the two species do interbreed which makes life difficult for the angler. Sometimes a hybrid is thought to be a specimen roach and can only be told apart from the proper fish by experts.

The rudd is a shoal fish which behaves similarly to the roach, but is found almost exclusively in still waters. It grows just slightly larger than the roach, and rudd of over 3 pounds (1·35 kg), although by no means common, are more often caught.

A catch of average-sized carp. They can grow much larger and some anglers dedicate all their fishing time trying to catch a large specimen.

A fine catch of rudd, tench and bream weighing 65 pounds in all. The rudd, at the top of the picture, are very similar to roach but are more golden in colour; they are not as common as roach.

The common carp is a deep-bodied fish covered with scales.

Carp Much mystery surrounds the carp. Because of its great size it is fanatically sought by some anglers using secret baits and in secret places. It is now stocked in some still waters at specimen size, but it is often caught in slow-moving rivers. It may be caught on the bottom of the water or at the surface. Baits are usually freelined because the carp picks up a bait from the bottom and runs with it, and if struck too early the bait may be pulled from its mouth.

Most of the carp caught now are mirror carp like this: the common English carp (or wild carp) is not at all common today. The mirror carp which were introduced from Europe have large scales dotted along their flanks.

Slipping a bream back into the water. This picture clearly shows the fish's characteristically humped back, which makes it easy to recognize.

Varieties of carp include the common, the leather and the mirror carp. The common carp has scales all over compared with the leather which has no scales, while the mirror has large scales along its flank. It is a powerful fish, not only because of its size, and will test any tackle to the full. The kind of baits that are used for carp are half-boiled potatoes, beans, sweet corn and mixtures of pet foods. It can also be taken on the common baits such as bread, maggots and worms. As with the chub it will take floating crust, which is really very exciting and rewarding. It reaches the same sort of weight, roughly, as the pike. There is almost a language of its own for carp fishing. A 'double' is a carp of 10 pounds (4·5 kg) and more, with a 'twenty' being a carp of over 20 pounds (9 kg). A really good specimen is over 20 pounds but many of more than 30 pounds (13·5 kg) are caught each season. The crucian carp is the small member of the carp family. It is a strong fish with habits which are the same as the other members of the carp family but is not as widespread. It is also popular as a fish with which to stock ornamental fish ponds.

Bream In recent years the bream has become a popular fish. Again it is a fish found in still waters and slow moving rivers, and is a bottom feeder. Large shoals of bream move slowly through chosen areas of the water, mopping up all food as they go. It is possible to hold a shoal in one spot with the use of groundbait, and then a very large catch of bream may be had. It is commonplace in some waters to catch more than 100 pounds (45 kg) of bream. Ireland and Denmark have many such waters, and some dedicated anglers travel regularly to these countries

The crucian carp is a much rounder fish than the common carp, and does not have fleshy barbules round its mouth. It never grows very large.

The silver bream is smaller and far less common than the ordinary bronze bream.

The bream is a deep-bodied fish which has flat sides and a humped back.

just for the bream fishing.

Even though it is a bottom feeder the bream often gives away its presence by rolling on the surface, and some expert bream anglers say that when they see bream rolling, they can always catch them. The more usual baits are bread, maggots and worms. Specimen bream are over about 7 pounds (3 kg) in weight with anything over 10 pounds (4·5 kg) being exceptional.

Silver bream A fragile-looking fish, the silver bream is a small version of the common or bronze bream with similar feeding habits. It is a much smaller fish than the common bream and is recognizable by its silver appearance, as its name suggests, and its red, grey-tipped pectoral and pelvic fins.

Dace This is another sleek fish with a silver finish and is attractive in its delicate appearance. Dace are mistaken for small chub, but the chub's fins have convex edges while those of the dace are concave. It does not grow very large by comparison with other species; a dace of more than 1 pound (0·45 kg) is a specimen. But many anglers fish for dace, because with light tackle they put up a dashing fight; a perfect dace of good size is a joy to see. It is not as widespread as the chub.

Barbel The barbel (like carp and some other species) has its fanatical specimen hunters, and rightly so. It is not a widespread fish but has been successfully introduced into some rivers such as the Severn where it is now very common. The most famous of all barbel rivers is the Hampshire Avon, followed by the Thames.

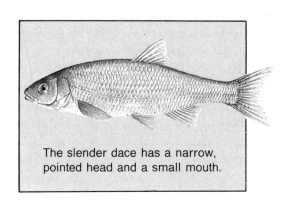

The slender dace has a narrow, pointed head and a small mouth.

19

These barbel were caught on the Thames. Barbel are great fighters, and you need strong tackle to fish for them successfully. They live in fast-running water, and weir-pools are good places to try for them.

The barbel is a really handsome fish, golden in colour and sleek in shape. It lives only in running water, no matter how deep or how fast, and the larger specimens often come from weir pools. Its mouth is on the underside of its body with feelers called barbules at the side. It usually feeds on the bottom and will take a variety of baits. A dead minnow is often successful but the more common bait is luncheon meat or sausage meat, and sweet corn is often used. It will take worms and maggots and cheese paste.

The barbel is a heavy fish and will make full use of the current of the river to help its already powerful resistance. A double-figure barbel is not rare but is a specimen fish, and would delight any specimen hunter. The largest barbel ever caught was foul-hooked by an angler spinning for salmon and was out of season. Nothing close to 20 pounds (9 kg) has ever been recorded.

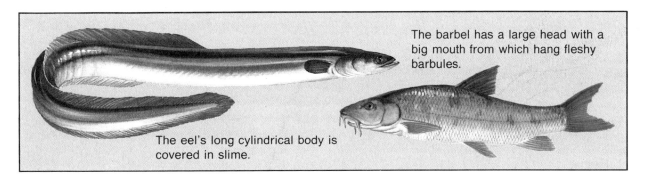

The barbel has a large head with a big mouth from which hang fleshy barbules.

The eel's long cylindrical body is covered in slime.

Eel Everyone knows the shape of an eel; in everyday language people are described as being 'as skinny as an eel', and so on. If you catch an eel (unless you are prepared for it) you will normally have a problem on your hands. The eel twists and turns and will tangle tackle in expert fashion. It will slide through holes in landing nets and is impossible to grasp with bare hands; it slips through like a bar of wet soap. It can also inflict a nasty bite. There are many suggested ways of dealing with eels but if you are inclined to keep one for the pot, just pop it into a sack and tie the neck. If you prefer to return the fish and you cannot grip the hook with forceps to remove it, just cut the line as near to the mouth of the fish as possible and set it free.

An eel will take all manner of baits, being a scavenger, but dead fish and worms and sometimes maggots are most used. Although small eels are a real nuisance, a big eel is a different matter and to land one is a great challenge. It is cunning and powerful and is very difficult to stop once it has made up its mind to reach snags in the water. It can be caught literally anywhere and an eel of over 4 pounds (1.8 kg) is regarded as a specimen.

This eel, weighing over 5 pounds, was caught on the Grand Union Canal using lobworms as a bait. Eel fishing is often done at night, when they are most active. They make very good eating and both elvers (as young eels are called) and fully grown eels are fished commercially.

A zander caught in the East Anglian Fen district. These fish are hard fighters and, like the pike and perch which they resemble, feed on smaller fish.

Zander This fish has had a lot of blame heaped on it for the poor fishing which came about in East Anglia soon after its introduction from the Netherlands. It is sometimes called a pike-perch, but is related to neither fish. It does have a spiny dorsal fin like a perch, but does not really look anything like a pike. It has now become fairly widespread in the Fens and the Midlands both because it has spread naturally and because it has been introduced illegally into other waters. It is a prolific breeder and will live in still water as well as rivers.

The zander is a scavenger and is caught on live and dead baits. It is also good to eat and to take the odd zander for the pot is common. The methods of fishing for the zander are the same as for pike and the two fish often feature in a day's fishing. It is a hard fighter when it reaches the larger sizes and is a wily fish. A double-figure zander is a good fish indeed and the zander record is forever increasing as it becomes more established in British waters.

Small and greedy

The gudgeon grows to just a few ounces, so it is not actively fished for by anglers – although of course in match fishing all fish are gratefully placed in the keep-net. It feeds only on the bottom and will make a nuisance of itself by nibbling away large baits, but will take maggots whole. Even though it may make a nuisance of itself, you should remember that on some days it is better to have a bite from a gudgeon than no bite at all, and so it should be treated with the respect that all fish deserve.

There are a number of varieties of loach. It is smaller than the gudgeon, though similar in appearance; its mouth, which has feelers on each side, is on the underside of its body. Like the gudgeon it lives only in flowing waters and will brave swift currents as easily as it will slow waters. As with the gudgeon, the loach feeds on practically any bait, especially maggots and worms.

Sometimes called a pope, the ruffe is another one of those nuisance fish that greedily takes a bait that is intended for a much bigger fish. It is shaped like a perch but grows to just a few ounces, and in comparison with the perch is drably coloured. It is brown, with spots on the spiny dorsal fin. It usually takes worms and maggots, and very often a tool called a disgorger is required to remove the hook because it swallows the bait so greedily.

Bleak is another very small fish that is sometimes found in still waters and is very common in rivers. It

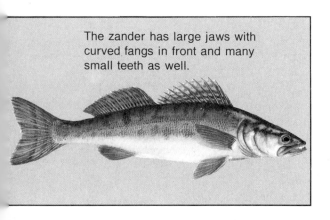

The zander has large jaws with curved fangs in front and many small teeth as well.

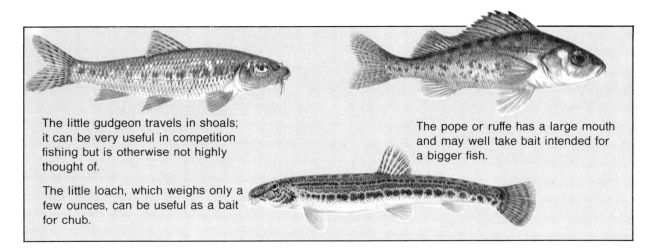

The little gudgeon travels in shoals; it can be very useful in competition fishing but is otherwise not highly thought of.

The little loach, which weighs only a few ounces, can be useful as a bait for chub.

The pope or ruffe has a large mouth and may well take bait intended for a bigger fish.

is a sleek, bright silver fish which is even smaller than gudgeon and loach. It tends to stay near the surface of the river, and trotting maggots or bread will account for bleak in large numbers if they are present.

Crossbreeds

The fish we have talked about are the types more usually found in British waters. There are of course other species, some more often found than others; and there are also hybrids of two or more species. For instance, bream and roach or rudd will crossbreed and produce a hybrid which can easily be mistaken for a very large roach; its correct identity can only be told by experts. Fortunately these hybrids are not very common and the species have to be closely related for the inter-breeding to occur. It should not be necessary to kill a fish to identify it. A clear photograph together with a sample of the scales of the fish should be enough for an expert to be able to tell just what it is.

A roach-bream hybrid; people often mistake this for a large roach. An expert will be able to identify it from a clear photograph and a few scales.

Rods, Reels and Lines

The most essential part of an angler's equipment is the rod. It can be made of various materials; the two most commonly used today are glass fibre and the more expensive light-weight carbon fibre. Depending on the type of fish which are sought, the rod can be powerful or sensitive; it can be very long or comparatively short. It is best to start fishing with an all-purpose rod and to add to your tackle collection as and when you are able.

All-purpose rods

The best all-round length for a rod to be used for a variety of fish is about 11 feet (3·3 m). An all-purpose rod of this length made of hollow glass fibre need not be at all expensive, and you might find one very cheaply in a second-hand shop; but make sure that it is what you really need by asking advice from someone who is able to help.

Fish such as carp, pike and barbel all require a powerful rod, the carp and pike more so not only because of their bulk and power, but also because in

A tackle shop will provide everything you need in bewildering variety. Take advice on what you will need to begin with; it is best to start with an all-purpose rod and to build up your collection as and when you can afford to.

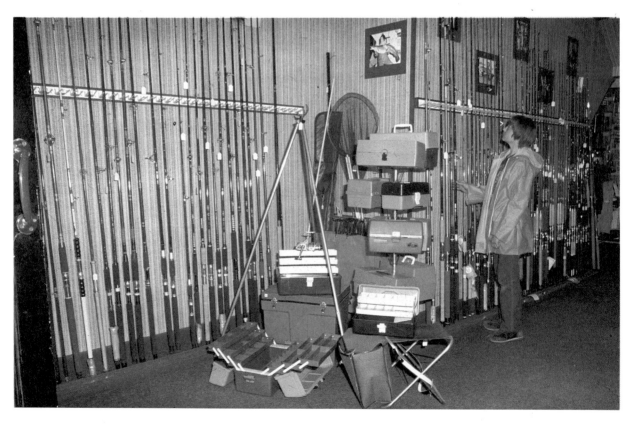

fishing for them quite large baits may have to be cast long distances. Most carp rods will bend so that the tip and butt are at a right-angle when supporting a weight of $1\frac{1}{2}$ pounds (0.68 kg). More powerful rods, known as 'stepped-up' carp rods, are used for big fish or for casting heavy baits for pike. Most are about 10 feet (3 m) in length.

Another factor which can affect the power of a rod is the number of rings along it through which the line is threaded, and how these rings are spaced. Too many rings on a rod will make it 'floppy' but will also make the rod bend all the way down its length, which is not necessarily a bad thing. Too few rings on a rod will also mean that it will not cast so well, because the line running through the rings will 'flap'. This puts friction on the line, and as a result the cast will not be as long or as accurate as it should have been. Your rod is purely a personal choice but it can affect your fishing drastically, so choose with care.

Rods for different uses

Short spinning rods (see page 48) are sold but are not really necessary. It is thrilling to catch a pike using a short spinning rod, but unless a heavy lure is used the casting distance will not be so great with a short rod. (Of course this is not always important; when fishing smaller rivers a long cast is not necessary, and many very good fish are caught with a short cast anyway.) A spinning rod is not a good all-round rod; if it is short it will not be ideal for float fishing (see page 44), and if it is longer then it will not be sensitive enough for float fishing.

Legering rods (see page 46) tend to be powerful rods because they are used for casting lead weights and loaded swimfeeders, sometimes for long distances. They sometimes have a spring-loaded piece at the tip which is used to detect shy bites from fish such as chub and barbel or roach. The spring-loaded piece has rings and the line is threaded through in exactly the same way as an ordinary tip section. Another feature of a leger rod is a tip ring which has a screw thread at the end of it. This is to enable you to screw in a spring tip or swing tip. The length of a leger rod can vary greatly; it can be short and powerful or longer with a softer 'through action'. The term through action means that the rod bends all through its length. A rod with a 'tip action' bends more easily at the tip than the butt, and 'butt action' means the reverse.

Float-fishing rods can be, and usually are, much lighter than legering rods. They should have a faster

Above: Even the simplest home-made rod like this will catch some fish. Its job is to present a bait to fish in the water by the use of a line and hook. A proper rod will be a much better instrument; it will cast the line out into the water and absorb the shock of a fish pulling for freedom. It will be lighter and less cumbersome, so far easier to store, and to carry to the water-side.

Above: Two Nottingham style centrepin reels – the cheapest of all to buy.

Above right: Two fixed-spool reels – an inexpensive one, good for a beginner, and a larger and more expensive kind.

Reels can be fixed to the rod simply with sliding ring fittings; the great disadvantage of these is that they may work loose.

action, because the line needs to be taken up more quickly in float fishing. In legering the line is almost always tight to the rod and there will be little or no slack, but in float fishing there is more often slack line which has to be taken up before contact with the fish can be made. This means that the rod must necessarily be longer and has to be sensitive as well. Lines of a very light breaking strain are sometimes necessary and a rod which is not sensitive enough may allow a fish to break the line.

Reels

The reel is not such an obvious part of the angler's equipment as the rod, but it is just as important. The type of reel that you use must match up to the type of rod. For instance it would not be a good idea to use a multiplying reel with a float-fishing rod; a multiplying reel is at its most useful when casting heavy baits long distances. You should also make sure that your reel is not too heavy for your rod.

The traditional fishing reels were centrepin reels and these are still widely used. They have not really been greatly improved upon, even by modern technology. The main improvement is the use of lighter metals, instead of the solid brass or wood of the original centrepins. These reels consist simply of a drum which is on a central spindle. The line is pulled out by the weight of the cast and by the fish, and recovered (wound back) with a handle. The rate of recovery of the line depends on the thickness of the spindle, and sometimes a cage is constructed around the spindle so that the recovery rate is improved. The centrepin is used mainly for long trotting (allowing the bait to float down the river with the current) where a long cast is not necessary.

Fixed spool reels are the most popular for all types of fishing where bait or spinners are used. They have a fast recovery rate due to gears built around the handle. Most of them have 'open faces', with the line exposed, which means that greater distances can be cast than with the centrepin. They are fitted with a 'slipping clutch' which means that the reel will not wind in line if the pull of a fish or snag is so great that the line is in danger of breaking. The slipping clutch can be set at any breaking strain.

Multiplying reels are used widely for casting heavy baits. They are geared so that they have a very fast recovery rate and are not a good reel to begin with; it needs a practised hand to use a multiplier properly, and the tangles which can be achieved are horrendous!

There are a number of different types of fittings to hold the reel to the rod. The original fitting, still widely used, is a simple pair of metal or plastic rings which slide over the reel seat and hold it. The reel can work its way loose with this fitting, which is very tiresome if it drops off as you are playing a fish, or even if it drops in the water while you are fishing. With a screw fitting, the fitting is screwed on to the reel seat, and this holds the reel much more securely.

Lines

Lines are generally sold on 100-metre spools and today are made of nylon. They are graded by breaking strain; to start with, a breaking strain of 2 pounds (0·9 kg) is a good one for float fishing, and a 6-pound (2·75 kg) line is another good general one. You can buy more spools as you can afford them.

This fixed-spool reel is held securely to the rod with a screw fitting, which cannot work loose. It is an open faced reel, with the line exposed so that it spills freely over the edge of the spool. The bale arm – the thin, curved piece of metal that goes from one side of the front of the reel to the other – is opened when casting. It is closed when winding in the line, and guides it on to the spool.

A match fisher using a roach pole of the kind widely used on the continent, and particularly in France. It is about 20 feet long, without rings, and with the line simply attached to the tip. The float is manoeuvred down the current until a fish takes the bait and it is then simply swung into the angler's hands. Although the fish caught are not large, experts with these rods can catch a great many in a short space of time, which makes them good rods for competitions. This angler is just fitting the rod together.

Hooks, Floats and Nets

Another essential part of the angler's equipment is the hook, which is simply a device for catching fish with bait. Hooks come in different shapes and sizes and success often rests on the hook you choose. A hook that is too small can mean that large fish will not be hooked properly, or (since it is made of thin metal) it may not be strong enough to handle a big fish. The bend of a hook can vary and it may have a small or large barb – or even no barb at all. But in the main it is a hook and as such is a device for catching fish with bait.

Hooks may have a spade end – where you have to tie on the line with a special knot – or they have the usual eye, which is easier to use. The bend may be straight or *offset*, which means that when viewed from straight-on the point appears to be bent in a different way from the shank. There are gilt hooks, bronzed hooks and silver hooks, but all are more often than not simply a matter of personal preference. It is not very often imperative to use one particular coloured hook. As we have said, it is usually the size of the hook that is most important. The type of hook you use depends on the bait you are fishing with. A carp hook for instance is made of heavy wire, suited to large baits. A treble hook, with three hooks brazed together, may be used for deadbait fishing for pike, zander and sometimes eels. Occasionally a treble hook is used when chub fishing, because the extra hooks help to hold a slightly soft bait, and very infrequently it is used in barbel fishing. Most spinners and plugs have one or more treble hooks attached to them.

An off-set hook (left), a treble hook (centre) and a gilt hook. Your choice of hook will make a big difference to the number of fish you catch.

A snap-tackle, ready made up as used for pike fishing. You can make up your own snap-tackle with the use of a wire trace and treble hooks. These days many anglers are using treble hooks without barbs, because of the terrible damage a number of barbed hooks in a fish at one time can do. Barbless hooks are also far easier to remove.

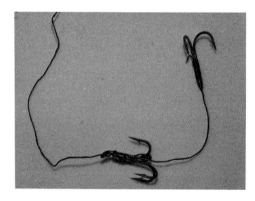

Different sizes of split shot; you will need all of these in order to be able to shot your floats correctly. A container like this makes it very easy to find exactly what you want. Fishing is always easier when you can keep things tidy.

Floats

A float is attached to a fishing line to hold the bait at the right depth. It bobs down when a fish takes the bait, showing the angler that a fish has bitten. The float is not an absolutely essential item for the angler; it is possible to fish without it. A wide variety of floats is available. The deciding factor when choosing which float to use should be the amount of shot required to cock it, that is to make it stand up in the water without actually sinking beneath the surface. A float which requires quite a lot of shot will cast farther than one that is lightly shotted. But it would not be wise to use a float with a bulky body to fish a tiny bait like a single maggot; a small float then makes much more sense because the fish would not feel the resistance of the float.

Quill floats are very good all-round floats. Whether the float is attached to the line at the top *and* the bottom or not depends on the water being fished and the conditions. Generally a float that is attached by the bottom ring only will be less disturbed by the wind than if two points are used to secure it to the line, because it sinks the line beneath the surface.

Sliding floats are used to fish very deep water. A stop on the line is used to stop the float from sliding farther than is needed and so that the bite of a fish will be indicated when the float hits the stop. The stop can be a knot, a matchstick or some other item attached to the line, but the important factor is that it must go through the rod rings when casting.

Nets

Every angler should have two nets, a landing net and a keep net. The landing net is used to land a fish that has been played out, so that the angler is able to unhook it. The keep net is a long net with a series of hoops which allow fish to swim freely within it until they are returned to the water at the end of the day. Modern substances are used which allow a net to be made without knots, as these damage fish by knocking off their scales and splitting their fins. A small mesh net is very much better than one with a large mesh.

The size of the net you buy will depend on its cost and the use to which you will put it. For example it would be no use trying to land a 20-pound (9 kg) carp or pike in a net with small rim. A large net always makes landing fish very much easier. A landing net with an extending handle is an advantage, especially when fishing from high banks or over obstacles such as reeds.

A selection of floats commonly used in coarse fishing. Such a selection would provide you with a float on most waters and under most conditions.

If you are after big fish, buy a big landing net like this, although it may cost more; many fish have been lost when the time came to net them because the net was too small. A large net will make it easy to land any fish.

Choosing Bait

These maggots for bait have been dyed to many different colours; the colour can make a difference to your catch.

The bait you use obviously depends totally on the species of fish which you are hoping to catch. There are two main categories: bait for predatory fish (those which live off smaller fish), and for non-predatory fish. There are one or two exceptions to the rule, particularly for the barbel which is generally regarded as non-predatory but which can be successfully fished for using dead minnows as bait.

Maggots are probably the most popular bait of all because there is no work involved in obtaining them – except on the part of the breeders. They are supplied by almost all tackle shops and come in a number of colours, natural, bronze and pink. Casters are just maggots that have reached the pupation stage and can also be an effective bait.

Worms are also popular because they can be obtained by digging the garden – a useful side effect for parents! The large type are lobworms. Brandlings and small red worms are usually found in manure heaps, and can be very effective bait.

Bread is also easy to get and use and is a good bait for those who like to keep their hands and fingernails clean. It can be used as breadflake (from the inside of

Two sorts of garden worms used for bait: lobworms, and the tiny brandlings. They are covered in earth in the bait box, to keep them alive.

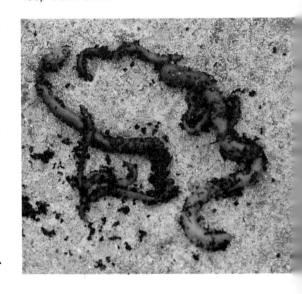

Breadflake, taken from the inside of a fresh loaf, has been pinched round a hook. It makes a cheap and easy bait for fish such as chub and carp on a large hook, or for roach on a small hook.

a new loaf), paste (stale bread mixed with water) or crust. It is a most successful bait for all bottom-feeding fish of the non-predatory type. Crust is usually used as a floating bait but can be fished anywhere in the water. Flake is simply pinched lightly around the shank of the hook so that it flakes out in the water, and is usually fished on the bottom.

Sweetcorn has become popular in recent years. It is simply the sweetcorn sold in tins in most grocery shops, and is used on the hook just as it comes out of the can.

Hemp is a very good bait for roach and often for barbel. It is not as popular as it was. Generally fish have to be taught to take it; the area to be fished is 'baited up' by introducing quantities of the boiled hemp seed into the water over a period of time. The fish learn to expect it and not fear it; they are lulled into a sense of false security. Some people claim that fish become addicted to the hemp and will no longer look at other baits, so hemp is banned in some waters.

This catch of roach and bream was taken on bronze maggots. Maggots are sold in tackle shops and should be kept in a tin with a perforated lid, in a cool place. They should be hooked through the blunt end, so that they remain lively in the water.

Mixing groundbait ready to start the day. The use of groundbait can be helpful, especially where fish such as bream and tench are in the area in large shoals. Sometimes the use of groundbait is not allowed, because some anglers tend to use too much; the groundbait which is not eaten by the fish affects the water. Groundbait can be of different types. There are those which feed the fish and those which attract them. The feeders are usually made up of breadcrumbs and are heavier; the lighter attractors sink slowly through the water, attracting the attention of the fish who are then supposed to find the hook bait. The type of bait being used on the hook can be mixed with the groundbait.

Wheat, like hemp, has to be boiled, and it also has to be introduced into the water before it is used as a hook bait.

Deadbaits are used for predatory fish and can be any sort of dead fish. Sea fish are very often used when fishing for any predatory fish, and especially pike and zander. Mackerel, herrings and sprats are mainly used; these are oily fish and are easily found by those fish that hunt partly by smell. Mackerel and herring may be a little large for eels but sprats are good deadbait for them. Freshly killed freshwater fish of a suitable size, usually roach or some non-predatory species, are also used as deadbait. Perch can be used if they are small. Treble hooks are used with the larger deadbaits; the usual way to mount them is with two trebles, one at the head of the fish and the other nearer the tail. When a fish takes a deadbait, give it a certain amount of time before striking because fish do not eat the bait straight away. Small deadbaits are usually threaded on to the line with the aid of a baiting needle.

Particle baits are mixtures of various items and are individual concoctions, usually invented by the angler who uses them. You will come across them most often when carp fishing. All sorts of ingredients are used – cat foods and trout pellets to name two.

Cheese is a highly successful bait in the right conditions, particularly for chub and barbel. Soft cheese is best, and it is a bait that is best when legered. It is kneaded into the required shape and size and then placed on the hook. Cheese paste is a mixture of cheese and bread kneaded together.

Meat of certain types is often used for chub and barbel, the two most popular being sausage meat and luncheon meat. These are cut in pieces and legered.

Wasp grubs can be bought from time to time. They are an excellent bait for most species of fish, and particularly for chub. It is, of course, a very risky business to try to obtain your own wasp grubs.

Insects of various sorts are used from time to time as a 'surprise' bait for some fish. It is usually the wily old chub that is subjected to bombardment with a number of curious baits such as bees and grasshoppers. **Slugs** are also used as an unusual bait for those crafty chub that have seen most other baits.

Cheese, bread and macaroni all prove popular baits; roach and chub, among other fish, will take them readily. It is worth trying other things from the kitchen shelves, like the dried peas and rice also shown here.

Crayfish are an excellent bait when freelined down the stream to chub living in places that are difficult to reach. They can be caught by placing meat or fish over a sieve or similar object which is then laid on the bed of the river where crayfish live. Once the crayfish have begun to attack the bait, the sieve is lifted and, with luck, the crayfish will be trapped on the sieve. The hook is inserted through a tail joint of the crayfish, which can be used alive or dead.

Minnows, which are plentiful everywhere, become food for most fish at some stage or another. They may be trapped and can be used alive or dead, as bait for perch, pike, eels, chub, barbel and others. A single hook about size 8 is all that is needed to fish a minnow, and it can be legered or float-fished.

Groundbait is not necessarily, and usually is not, the bait that is used on the hook. It is scattered into the water while fishing to keep the fish feeding in a particular area – in front of you. It should be something that will interest the fish but not feed them to the extent that they are no longer interested in your hook bait.

Loose feeding is simply throwing in the odd piece of hook bait now and again to keep the interest of the fish. Just odd pieces of bread or a few maggots are all that is needed to attract fish to the area.

A swimfeeder is a hollow plastic tube with holes in it, which can be used to replace the leger weight. Weights can be added to it. The tube is packed with the hook bait, which gradually makes its way through the holes and attracts the fish. This swimfeeder contains maggots; some have already wriggled their way out.

Even in summer it is sensible to take a light jacket or a jersey or two, as sitting still in a breeze can be decidedly chilly. A peaked hat keeps the sun out of your eyes; many anglers wear dark glasses to cut the glare and help them see just what is happening on the water. This angler is wearing a waterproof jacket with large pockets, and waders which are expensive but very useful on marshy banks and in other difficult places.

What to Wear

The only thing that is worse than going fishing and not catching fish – or even getting bites – is to do so and be uncomfortable! If you feel the cold or forget waterproof clothing, and it rains, you will not be able to concentrate as you can when you feel relaxed. So make sure that you have clothing that will protect you against the weather when you are fishing.

Warm and comfortable
It is a good idea to wear several layers of clothing. This will allow you to peel off a jersey or two if you are too warm, while on a cold day two or three medium-weight jerseys will keep you much warmer than one thick one.

The sort of outer clothing that you wear will depend entirely on how much you can afford. It is possible to spend a lot of money on a coat and

Everybody who fishes does quite a lot of bending forward when un-hooking or landing fish, putting the fish in the keep net and so on. It is really very important, during the colder months of the year, to make sure that you wear a long shirt and jumpers that will keep your back covered and warm. There is nothing worse than having to keep undoing a waterproof coat to tuck in a troublesome shirt. You should remember always that if you are comfortable it will help your fishing a great deal.

These anglers are well wrapped up for a cold day's fishing. They are wearing layers of jerseys (several layers of lighter jerseys keep you warmer than one very thick one) and sturdy waterproof boots with non-slip soles. One has a waterproof jacket. You are likely to fish much better if you are warmly and comfortably dressed.

There is no need to spend a lot of money on clothes when you start fishing; these children are wearing ordinary windproof jackets while 'moonboots' are waterproof and comfortable. More serious fishermen might prefer to avoid bright colours which fish could catch a glimpse of.

overtrousers and it is also possible to buy them cheaply. They will do the same job for you, but usually the cheaper items are not so long lasting. The most expensive outer clothing is what is known as waxed cotton. This will stand up to all sorts of hard wear and will last for some time. At the other end of the scale there are the thin nylon type of outer clothes. These are all very well for ordinary rambling, but remember that you will be walking through brambles and getting caught on tree branches, and anything like this will soon rip clothing that is not heavy enough to withstand it. If you are lucky your local tackle shop will be able to help, while some agricultural merchants sell waterproof clothing of the kind used by farmers at very reasonable prices.

Waterproof footwear

Ordinary rubber boots should be quite good enough when the banks are muddy and the grass is wet. There are not many waters that make it really necessary for you to wear waders in order to fish, so you should be able to do without these. Whatever you choose in the way of waterproof boots, do make sure that they have very good grips on the sole. You will certainly have to climb up and down river banks and you will not be able to do so safely if your feet will not grip properly. And make sure that you have good socks inside to make the boots warmer and more comfortable.

Assembling Tackle

A complete set of tackle will cost quite a lot of money but it can, fortunately, be built up over a period of time. You must buy wisely, otherwise you will spend your money on replacing worn out items and you will not be able to afford to add to your collection. We have already covered the subject of rods and reels and clothing, but there are other items of tackle that you will need almost as much, and certainly every bit as much if you want to enjoy your fishing to the full.

Hold-alls

Obviously an important item of tackle is a hold-all – which is better thought of as a 'carry-all' because, don't forget, you will have to carry this when you are walking to your fishing swim, wearing your clothing, and it will contain all your tackle. It is possible to use just a haversack which is very convenient; but then you will also have to carry something on which to sit. Too many items of tackle to carry can make things very awkward, especially when you have to open gates and wade across little streams. The very best that you can do is to buy a rigid box made of fibreglass, or a metal-framed box covered with a form of pvc, which you can pack things into and then sit on when you reach your destination. Buy it as large as you can afford, or as large as you can carry.

If you have more than one rod plus rod rests and so

This float box keeps a good selection of floats in order; it is not difficult to make a simpler version for yourself. One of the floats in it was used to catch the tench in front of it.

Starting the day. The rod holdall and the tacklebox, which can be used to sit on, make carrying much easier.

This angler has laid out his tackle around him, making it easier to find things. An umbrella makes a useful shelter against the wind. Now the tackle hamper he used to carry his tackle makes a good seat.

Think carefully before buying and remember that although the most expensive items are not always the best they are always worth considering. Usually there is an item at a 'middle-of-the-road' price that will last you for a long time and will do the job well. Don't be afraid to ask!

on, a rod hold-all is a good idea. These vary a great deal in price and you should be able to find one quite cheaply that will suit you to begin with. If you continue fishing, you will undoubtedly have to buy a bigger one at a later date.

Umbrellas for shelter

A good umbrella will certainly make fishing in the rain or in bitter winds a very much more comfortable occupation and, as we have already said, you will definitely fish better if you are comfortable. The size of the umbrella is of more importance than its actual construction, and the larger it is the better it will serve you. Don't forget to have some cord with you which can be used to anchor the umbrella in position and keep it from being blown away.

Bank sticks are very useful items to have in your rod hold-all. A bank stick is a short metal pole with a point at one end and a screw thread at the other, and is used to hold your keep-net in position. It can also be used as a rod rest. The screw thread used in fishing tackle tends to be the same for all the different items of tackle.

Putting tackle together on the banks of a canal. This is a job which must not be hurried; a small slip can cost you a big fish. Test all knots when you have finished tying them; if they come loose, you may lose not only a fish but also some expensive tackle.

When a float like this is shotted correctly, the main body should be beneath the surface with just part of the top 'antenna' showing. As you can see, this float has been undershotted and as a result it can be blown about by the wind.

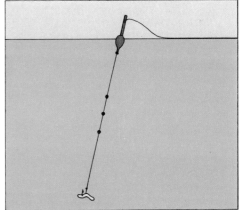

Putting it Together

Putting your tackle together at the riverside should be a fairly elementary task, but it is often easy to overlook some small point which might mean that you lose the fish of a lifetime. Firstly, you will save your rod a lot of wear if you keep metal ferrules lightly greased. Glass-fibre spigots should be kept greased with candle wax, by simply rubbing a candle over the spigot. Not only will doing this prevent wear

Right: Some common knots, and how they are tied. Tie your knots loosely and tighten them gently, but not completely, then wet the line and firmly pull the knot together while the line is still wet. Never hurry the tying of a knot; you will probably end up taking longer and it may still not be well done.

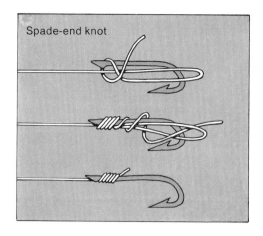

Spade-end knot

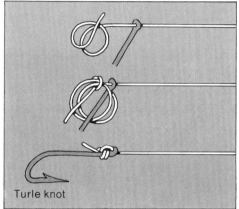

Turle knot

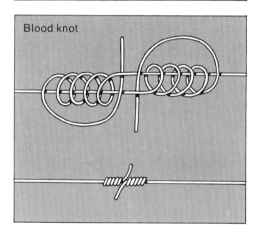

Blood knot

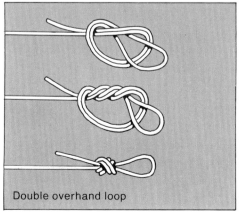

Double overhand loop

on the rod; it will also ensure that you will be able to pull the sections apart easily at the end of the day. When assembling your rod, if it is more than two pieces long, join the top section to the middle section first, and then the middle to the butt section last. Take the rod apart in the reverse order.

Reels and rings

Just where you place your reel on the handle is a matter of personal preference. It should be far enough up the handle to balance the rod, but not so far that the butt catches you when you are casting. Threading the line through the rings is very straightforward but should not be hurried. It is too easy to be ready to fish and then find that a ring has been missed through haste, and it means that you have to start all over again.

Adding the float

The next step is to add your float to the line, which is straightforward in most cases. A float with a ring at the bottom and a rubber at the top should have the line inserted through the rubber first from above and then through the ring at the bottom, and it should then be slid up the line out of the way. A float to be secured only by the bottom ring can be tackled in two ways. The first is to pass the line through the ring twice. This can make adjusting the depth difficult, and if you hook a large fish the tightness of the line when you play it may cause the ring to cut through the line. The safest and most convenient way is to add a rubber just above the ring, from the bottom, and then thread the line through in the same way that you would if you were securing the line top and bottom.

Shotting the float

The next step is to shot the float correctly. The position of the shot in relation to the float and the hook depends on where and how you are fishing. The float should not stand up too high in the water as this will make it easy for the wind to blow it around and any shy bites will not be shown clearly. It is better to shot the float so that not much at all shows above the water, but if you do so in the first instance and then use a heavy bait, like a worm, the float will sink; so you have to think about it carefully if you are to get it right first time. Pinch the shot gently on to the line. Do not bite it on; this flattens the line and can weaken it. It also makes it very difficult, if not impossible, to remove the shot at the end of the day.

Where to Go?

When you have collected together your fishing tackle you must take the great decision where to go to catch fish. Some of us are more fortunate than others and may have a number of choices, although this is not always a good thing because we can be spoilt for choice! What you must take into consideration is what fish you hope to catch, and what the weather conditions are like and have been over the past few days.

The most important thing of all is to make sure that you will be safe wherever you fish. That means taking a companion with you and making sure that people know where you are going, just in case of any accidents or in case you are needed while you are away. Time always passes very quickly when fishing and it is not fair to allow people to worry unnecessarily.

Still or flowing?

As we have said, fish can be found in the most surprising places and many small ponds hold fish. There are usually some lakes or gravel pits which hold fish near to most homes, and rivers flow through every county in England, Wales, Scotland and Ireland. Rivers can be more interesting because there is always something happening in them, since the

Float fishing slack water at the side of a weir-pool. An amazing number of species of fish can be taken in weir-pools, and they are fished particularly for barbel and chub. Although water in a weir-pool is tumbling from a higher level and then racing away, not *all* of the water is moving that fast. It is usually only the surface water that is moving, while if the pool is deep the water at a deeper level will be comparatively quiet – but well oxygenated, which is very important for fish. Eddies at the edge of the weir-pool can be float-fished, but the most effective way of fishing the main pool is to leger.

The river Thame, here scarcely more than a stream. But such small rivers often provide very good fishing.

Fishing a typical chub swim. The chub are attracted by the roots of the willow trees, which reach out into the water and provide shelter both for the chub and for the creatures on which they feed. In such surroundings they are often to be found near the bank, and a legered bait may well tempt them out. If the first bait that you try does not succeed, try something different. Luncheon meat or cheese sometimes work better than other baits which the fish may have seen regularly used by other anglers.

current will keep your tackle on the move. However, they are not always the best places to fish. Heavy rain over a period of time will make the water very coloured because it washes the mud off the land into the river and, although the fish will still feed under these conditions, they are not usually as ready to do so as they would be if the water was clearer and the current not so swift. On the other hand, if there has been no rain for a long period the fish may again be difficult. There are happy mediums and the only way that you will find them is by fishing the same waters often.

Lakes and gravel pits can be affected by rain. The extent to which this happens depends on their size and depth. The thing that affects fish most of all is temperature. Fish are cold blooded, which means that their temperature is the same as that of the water, and when the water is cold they do not feed

Fishing for pike at Sywell Reservoir near Northampton. The large float is used specially for pike fishing. Reservoirs are very popular places for fishing and often provide good catches.

Eddies are like slow whirlpools; you can see the characteristic ripples on the water in the foreground of the picture. Fish feed on the food and rubbish which gather there.

heavily all the time. Instead they tend to feed for a short time and then rest. This is why a lot of cold rain will have the effect of reducing the feeding activities of the fish.

Which water?

Having chosen where it is you are going to fish, you then have to make the additional decision of just where on that water you are going to start fishing. With rivers, you may base your choice on the type of fish you would like to catch. The basic choices of water that you will have on every river are fast water, slack water and eddies, as well as deep and shallow water. Eddies are usually a very good bet for catching a variety of different species of fish. You would be likely to catch roach, perch, chub and pike and many others there. An eddy is usually formed where the current changes direction. It is like a very slow whirlpool in which food and rubbish collect, and so do the fish because they do not have to fight the stronger current to find their food. You will find eddies quite often on all rivers, and the most productive part of the eddy usually is right on the edge of the faster water.

There will always be obstacles wherever you fish, whether it is lake or river, and if the water is deep enough there will be fish of some kind around them. The fish that prefer to live among the snags and obstacles are the predators, particularly chub, pike and perch. They use them for cover to hide in until they come out to strike their prey. They are difficult to land, if they are of any size, once they have been hooked because they dive back into their lair if you allow them to.

Food and shade
Overhanging branches shelter places that hold fish, particularly during summer, because insects drop from them and they also provide shade. They are easy to fish beneath in rivers because you can float your bait down to them, but more difficult on still waters where you have to rely on the accuracy of your casting to be able to place your bait close enough to them to tempt the fish out. Lily pads must be every angler's favourite feature on any water. They provide shade for the fish, grow in deep water on muddy bottoms and harbour lots of food. Rushes and reeds always look inviting but this can be deceiving, particularly on rivers.

Anything that provides cover, and possibly food, for the fish is worthy of consideration and sometimes large fish turn up in the most unlikely places. Never be afraid to try something different, because the bigger fish have usually seen every normal type of tackle and tactics and it is often something unusual that tempts them.

The larger, the deeper
As a rough guide you will find that the larger fish tend to prefer deeper water, and the smaller species will be found in faster water as well as slow. The wind will have more bearing on your fishing in still water than it will on the rivers, because it is the wind that affects the temperature of the water most on still waters while the current affects it on rivers. If the air temperature is colder than the water temperature and the wind is strong, the fish will be found in greater numbers on the windward side – that is the side from which the wind is blowing. If the air temperature is warmer than the water with a strong wind the fish will be more likely to be on the leeward bank – the bank to which the wind is blowing. This is because the waves lapping the bank mix the water and either make it colder or warmer, depending on the temperature of the air; and fish, even though they are cold blooded, prefer to be warmer rather than colder. They also feed better when they are warmer.

An angler with two nice roach caught in a gravel pit. Gravel pits, like reservoirs, are man-made areas of water that provide good sport.

Float Fishing

Most anglers begin by float fishing. In this, the baited hook is kept in the right position in the water by passing the line through a float. When a fish takes the bait, the float dips below the surface and the angler knows the time for action has arrived.

The golden rule to observe when float fishing is to make sure that you do not use a float heavier than you have to. If you do not need to cast very far then a light float which does not need much lead will be best. If you are needing to cast a long way then a heavier, streamlined float will cast better because of its shape and the fact that you will need to use more lead to cock it properly. You should choose your float after deciding how much lead you will need to fish the bait properly.

Choosing a float

The early floats used in fishing were stems from the feathers of swans and peacocks. They were known as quill floats. Nowadays reed stems from foreign countries have taken the place of quill floats, and cork-bodied and balsawood-bodied floats are also popular. Many of them mark on their stems the number of shot that they will need to be cocked

Threading the line through the rings of a float is a fiddly job but it is important to get it right.

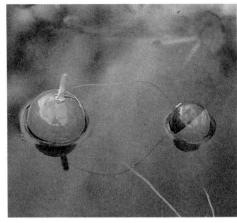

Pike fishing from a boat; the float can clearly be seen on the water. The picture below shows the special pike bung with a pilot float which is free-running on the line, and helps to prevent the floating line from tangling with the main float as the live bait tows it about.

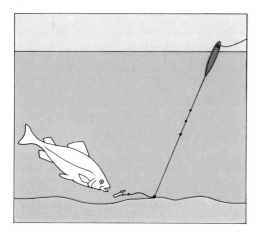

'Laying on' is used particularly in winter to tempt a lazy fish with a stationary bait. Set the float so that the distance between it and the bait is more than the depth of the water and place the shot as shown in the diagram. If you cast out across the current, the water will swing the tackle down to rest immediately downstream from your rod.

Rod, line and float; the line is resting on the surface of the water.

correctly (see page 39). This means that you will not have to stand over the water and experiment until you get it right.

Your tackle collection should include several different types of float in different sizes. Zoomers are used for casting longer distances; wind-beaters are used on windy days when other floats may be affected more by the surface drift caused by the wind; wagglers are used more on rivers, as are stick floats. Floats with bulbous bodies are used for heavy baits such as lobworms and deadbaits. They are used for fishing for predatory fish with mouths that may not be so sensitive, and that may not be so selective in the manner in which they take the bait. A fish that takes the bait gently, such as a roach or even a carp, will feel any resistance that a big float will give and will reject the bait long before you have the chance to set the hook firmly in the fish's mouth.

Setting the hook

The length of time that you are given in which to set the hook will depend on the bait. With baits such as maggots, sweetcorn and bread the float should be only just showing above the surface, and as soon as it disappears the strike (the pull on the line which will set the hook) should be made. In order to make sure that this is done quickly, you should never have more than just enough line on the water to reach the float (to leave extra line on the water will mean that the movement of the float will be affected by wind or current and make the bait look unnatural). This means that you will not have to do much more than flick your wrist to set the hook, which is ideal. Baits such as lobworms and deadbaits may be taken for some way by the fish before they are devoured, and so once the float has moved off and the line is moving through the water the fish should be stopped with a firm strike.

Useful dodges

Two simple dodges will help you in difficult conditions. When fishing faster water, or where the currents travel at different speeds, grease your line so that you can pick it up off the water by raising the tip of the rod without moving your float too much. Your float will then stay where you want it to. When you are fishing on a windy day and your float is constantly being blown out of position, use a float attached at the bottom only and dip your rod tip below the surface of the water so that your line is sunk between the rod and the float.

Legering

In legering the bait is presented on the bottom and held there by the means of lead weights through which the line is threaded. The lead weight is prevented from getting right to the hook by means of a stop between the hook and the leger. There is usually no float and so the only way that you will know that you have a bite is when the line moves at the rod. This is when you strike. The technique of legering can be fairly easy to master, particularly on still waters, or it can be infuriatingly difficult.

Choosing your weight

There are numerous types of leger weight and, as with other methods of coarse fishing, the type that you choose depends on the water that you fish. The most common weights which you will come across are the Arlesey bomb, bullet, coffin and barrel, and there are different weights of each type of leger. With these it should be possible to cover most situations, as described in the caption.

Spotting the bite

When you have chosen the water and the leger weight, you will have to give some thought to the method of bite indication. You will need at least one rod rest and more usually two, and it is most useful if they are adjustable in height. When fishing a 'rolling' leger in running water, it is best to use one rod rest with the rod raised on it. The leger is cast across the current and as it bumps across the bottom, tighten your line constantly; you will soon get to know which is the leger moving and which is a fish taking the bait.

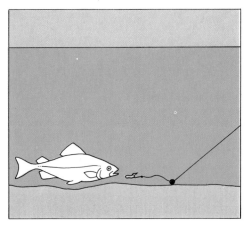

This diagram shows the basic principle of legering, though in fact it is a skilled business. Some fish will not readily take a bait with only a short link to the leger. (The link is the line between the hook and the leger weight.) Other fish are more likely to take a short-link leger. The length of the link makes a difference as to how the bait fishes in running water, while in still water it could determine whether the bait is pulled into mud or weeds by the leger weight.

A selection of leger weights. The Arlesey bomb (left) is the best weight for casting long distances and holds the bottom well. The flat, coffin-shaped weights are known as coffin leads; they hold the bottom in most conditions. In still waters they are less inclined than the others to sink into a muddy or silted bottom, because they have a greater surface area. Barrel leads (right) are shaped like a thin barrel and they have generally been overtaken by the Arlesey bomb. Bullet leads (not shown) are round weights drilled through the middle; they are ideal for searching the bottom in fast-moving water as they will roll along.

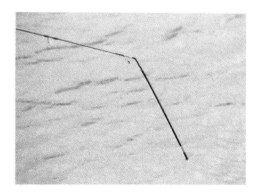

Above: A swing-tip bite indicator which screws into the top ring of a bottom-fishing rod.

Below: This bite indicator has been made simply from the top of a washing-up-liquid bottle.

A leger rod set up with two rod rests, and the swing tip at rest near the surface of the water to steady it.

If your leger weight is to remain stationary on the bottom you have a choice of bite indicators, depending on the bait. If you are fishing small baits or bread, a swing-tip will give you good indication of quick bites. A swing tip is an additional loose tip which screws into the end of a specially fitted ring on the tip of your rod. Your rod should be resting on two rests and the line tightened so that the rod points straight down the line. The line should be very nearly tight to the rod tip but allow just enough slack so that the swing tip can hang freely. When a fish takes the bait, the swing tip will lift upwards and if it stays there it is time to set the hook. A spring tip or quiver tip is just a spring-loaded version of the swing tip which is used in much the same way.

If you are using deadbaits or large baits such as you would for carp and eels, a bobbin indicator will be best. The line is tightened to the leger and then a bobbin is fixed to the line between the butt ring and the reel. The top from a washing-up-liquid bottle is ideal, as it is easily added to and removed from the line. The bale arm is then taken off the reel and just a little slack allowed so that the bite indicator hangs down. When a fish takes the bait the bobbin will lift to the rod, and if the fish runs with the bait it will be free to do so because the bale arm is off the reel.

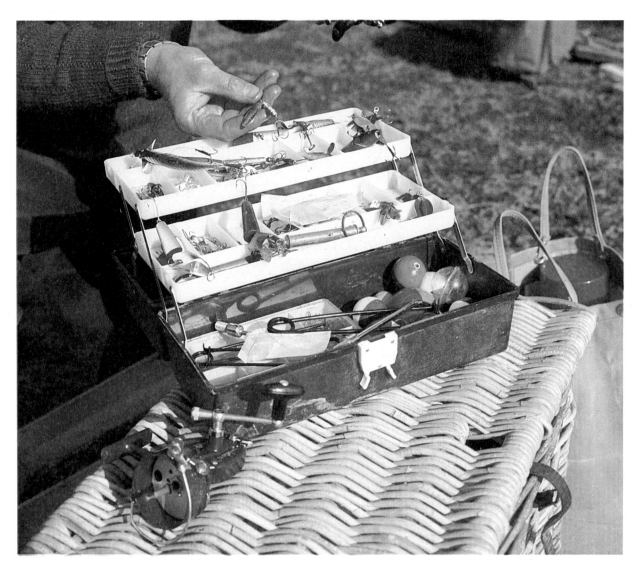

Spinning

Spinning is the use of an artificial lure, usually a spinner or a plug, which is designed to imitate some form of food or to attract the fish with its flash or colour. It is more commonly used to catch pike but other fish will readily take a spinner or plug, notably zander, perch and chub.

Spinning tackle is quite straight forward. A short rod and an ordinary fixed spool or multiplier reel can be used. You can spin and plug fish in rivers and still waters and in deep and shallow water, in fact anywhere that predators may be lurking.

Plugs and spinners
Plugs fall into different categories. There are jointed and non-jointed plugs – jointed ones tend to have

A useful collection of plugs and spinners. Their bright colours and the way in which they catch the light attract fish.

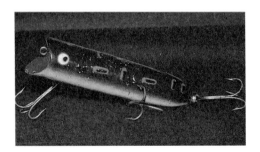

This plug has caught many pike, and you can see on it the marks made by their sharp teeth.

more movement, while the single-bodied ones usually move with a slow wobble. There are surface plugs which you retrieve over the surface in shallow water or over or near weeds, and diving plugs with a vane at the front which means that they dive when retrieved. Some even have adjustable vanes so that you can change the angle at which they dive. There are deep-diving plugs and shallow-diving ones, depending on how deep the water is that you will fish. The size depends on what you are fishing for and how far you need to cast.

The same basic principles apply to spinners, or spoons as they are also known. Some spin faster than others and some wobble and flash rather than spin. They are the ones that are used to attract the fish by flash rather than imitation.

Deep or shallow

The weight of a spinner can make the difference as to whether it fishes deep or shallow, and weights can be added to the line. The easiest way to fish deep with a spinner is to cast, allow sufficient time for it to sink and then retrieve slowly with the rod tip held down. If you want the spinner or plug to come in higher in the water, raise the rod tip and retrieve faster. The best places to spin are near weeds and obstacles and there is usually no need to strike as the fish tend to hit the lure hard and hook themselves. It is possible to spin deadbaits; this can be a killing method for predators which hunt by smell as well as sight, and it is used very often for pike and zander. The baits used most often are sprats which are mounted on a specially constructed spinning mount.

Spinning for pike on the fens. The bait is reeled back through the water, to imitate the movements of a small fish.

You can see the yellow spinner hanging from the end of the line, just below the level of the bridge. Perch, chub, zander and above all pike are caught by spinning.

Casting

Whatever method of fishing you use you must get your bait where you want it by casting it into the water. The main considerations when casting are the ability of the bait to withstand the force of the cast, and the accuracy required. You should only use as much force as is needed to reach the spot where you intend to fish, and the force should be put into the cast through the rod – in other words the action of the rod should do the casting for you.

Learning the action

With a two-handed rod, grip the butt end of the rod with one hand and then take a firm grip with the other hand up the rod above the reel. There should be just enough line hanging from the tip to swing the bait properly, but not so much that it swings uncontrollably. If you are using a fixed-spool reel, take the line under the index finger of your upper hand and take off the bale arm which guides the line on to the spool. Alternatively you can use your index finger against the spool to stop the line peeling off. Take the rod back and then bring it smartly forward so that it whips and when the tackle and bait have passed the rod tip, release the line that is trapped by your finger. As soon as your tackle hits the water take up the slack line.

Ready to cast; you can see the float hanging below the tip of the rod. Casting for coarse fish is quite different from making a fly-fishing cast (see page 70); there is no need to swing the line out behind you.

Casting into a stream. You can see the float just in front of the rod.

A good grip of the rod. The forefinger of your upper hand (the right, if you are right-handed) should be in a good position to trap the line against the edge of the spool – or against the rod's handle, as in this case – until just before the rod tip is in front of you, when you lift it and release the line.

At first you will find it easier to cast standing up, but as you gain experience you will be able to cast sitting down. If there is very little room behind you, try a sideways cast rather than the usual overhead movement.

You will find that your accuracy improves with practice, but it helps if when you are preparing for your cast you actually look at the spot where you want your tackle to be after the cast. If you are float fishing fairly deep or are using a soft bait, you can reduce the amount of force used by using more arm movement in the cast. If you are using a centrepin reel, you will not be able to cast as far as with a fixed-spool reel. The accepted method of casting is to peel line off the reel and then trap it as with the fixed-spool reel, releasing the line as before. The centrepin reel requires much practice before you can cast even reasonably well.

Multiplying problems

Casting with a multiplier reel also requires plenty of practice. The multiplier generally holds more line than other reels and recovers line faster. It has a free-running device which is brought into play when casting, and you use the rod in much the same way as with the fixed-spool except that with a multiplying reel you can use more force because it is used for spinning and deadbaiting. Watch the bait or spinner carefully with your thumb poised over the reel, and as soon as the bait hits the water stop the spool revolving by braking it with your thumb. Starting the retrieve will over-ride the free-running device. The tangles that occur with multiplier reels are usually overruns and are often horrific, being real 'birds' nest' tangles which take a long time to unravel.

The fixed-spool reel is easily the best reel for a beginner to learn to cast with and is the best all-round reel for coarse fishing.

Playing and Landing

Once you have hooked your fish you have to land it, which can be easy or difficult depending not only on the size of your fish but also on where you are fishing. The main problem you have is in actually tempting the fish to take the bait or lure, so concentrate on that first and then on how and where you will land it. For a start the fish may do something totally unexpected, so there is not a lot of point in making plans for the battle before it has begun.

Playing

The most useful tactic that you can use when you are playing a strong fish is sidestrain. This is just what it says it is; if your fish is running towards a tree root or weeds, for instance, lay the rod to one side and pull hard on the fish and it will probably turn. Once it has turned you can then apply pressure as normal. You should, wherever possible, keep your rod up and bent into the fish so that it acts as a shock absorber against the runs and turns of the fish.

Into the net

Assuming that you have beaten your fish, you must get its head up above the surface so that it slides across the surface to your waiting net. Wind in enough line so that when you lift the rod and bring your arm back, the net will reach the fish; sink the leading rim of the net beneath the surface and draw

A long-handled net makes it easier to land your catch. Remember not to lose your balance in the excitement; banks are slippery places so if you can, it is safest to remain seated like this angler.

A fish safely in the landing net. The fine mesh, without knots, does the least possible damage to the fish's scales. If the fish is to be set free, keep it in the net while you unhook it, to avoid unnecessary handling; then simply lower it into the water.

the fish over it. When the fish is over the net, lift the net and allow your line to go slack and then bring in your fish.

No hands

If you do not need to use a net but could swing in the small fish that you catch, it may still be best not to do so; this can easily damage the fish. To use a net is much the fairest thing to do for the fish and it means that you do not have to handle them. Handling a fish with dry hands removes the slime from them, and this is their only protection against deadly fungus growths that will attack them in the water when they are released. Try never to handle your fish but if you do have to, wet your hands first. If you leave fish in the landing net it will be possible to unhook them without handling them and it means that they can be kept more quiet as you unhook them. If you are transferring the fish to a keep net, the landing net will be useful to wet your hands with before you do.

When you are landing your fish, never stretch yourself because you will be off balance and then an accident could easily occur.

Before you start fishing you should set the slipping clutch on your fixed-spool reel so that a fish cannot break your line, but simply takes line from you – and if a fish does take line from you, never, ever wind against the clutch because this kinks your line and weakens it or causes tangles.

Back they go; a catch of fish is released into the water, perhaps to provide other anglers with sport in days to come. When you are releasing your catch, keep the lip of the net as close to the water as possible.

Fly Fishing

The only likeness between coarse fishing and fly fishing is that in both you have to find and then catch your fish. Both the tackle for fly fishing and the way in which you use it are very different.

In fly fishing, artificial flies made of fur, feathers, hair and other materials are used instead of bait. These are cast on to the water where you can see fish (particularly trout) feeding, or where you think they are likely to be. 'Dry' flies, which float on the surface, are cast a little upstream of the fish and allowed to float down on the current. 'Wet' flies sink below the surface. The flies are not left on or in the water for any length of time, but are pulled back (or retrieved) in movements which imitate those made by the real insects.

These flies weigh very little, and in order to cast them on to the water a much heavier line must be used than lines used in coarse fishing. The fly is joined to this heavy line by a lighter line known as a cast or leader, which varies in length according mainly to your own choice.

Stocking the waters

When you go coarse fishing, you look for whatever fish are living naturally in the waters you visit. But another great difference in trout fishing is that in most of the waters the fish have been stocked – trout bred in fish farms have been released into them, to join those breeding and living there naturally. This sort of fishing has developed over the last 20 years or so. Before that trout streams and rivers were mostly privately owned, or belonged to clubs, and in most places trout waters which anyone could go to had few fish in them. But then people began to stock reservoirs with fish and allowed anyone to fish there for a small fee. Now waters from huge reservoirs to small lakes are stocked with fish, where for a few pounds you can enjoy a day's fishing – and take home your catch. Salmon fishing remains too expensive for most people, so we have said little about it here.

It is not practical to use any of your coarse fishing tackle for fly fishing and so you will have to start a new collection. Work along the same lines as for coarse fishing, buying wisely and asking for advice wherever you might need it.

Left: Trout fishing on the river Kennet, one of England's most famous trout streams. Fishing streams like this is still the best of all ways of fly fishing, but it is expensive; today, many waters have been stocked with fish which makes it possible for anglers to enjoy a good day's fishing for only a few pounds.

Stocking a water with trout fresh from the hatchery. In this picture trout are being released by hand. Much larger amounts may be delivered by lorries into large still waters or large rivers. Whichever way they are released, they must be carefully looked after and provided with oxygen on their journey to the water.

Trout and Salmon

There are basically two types of trout commonly fished for with the fly in Britain – the brown trout, which is a native, and the rainbow trout, an immigrant which was introduced from America during the 19th century. Thanks to the enormous business interest which has been shown in trout fishing in the last 20 years or so, there are many types of fishing available to everyone and within easy reach of most parts of the country.

Trout will live in still water and in running water as long as it is not polluted or tainted. They will live in deep or shallow water, and in swift- or slow-running water. They are popular as a stock fish for this reason and because they are delicious to eat, which means that in the main you will have to pay more for your trout fishing than for coarse fishing.

Greedy feeders

Trout feed on a large variety of food – in fact they will eat almost anything that falls on to the water. They will even take cigarette ends and other bits of rubbish such as feathers that either fall or are thrown into the water. Trout have even been caught with stomachs full of duck feathers. Their varied feeding habits make trout popular with anglers, and the comparative lightness and convenience of the tackle used to catch them is another bonus. There is no fiddling to be done with baits, although you may have to make many changes of fly during the course of a day's trout fishing.

The native brown trout (top) usually has spots on its gill covers, whereas the rainbow trout (above) has silver gill covers, often tinged with pink. The rainbow has spotted fins and the brown does not. Another helpful indication is the colour; the rainbow is usually a much more silver fish. These general guides will help you to tell the difference between the two nearly every time.

The results of patience and endurance are fish such as this superb brown trout, caught by the author.

A very nicely marked brown trout from the river Torridge in Devon.

A fly fisher's dream: a fine collection of rainbow trout in shallows. They have probably gathered to spawn in which case they should be left in peace.

Although trout will take almost anything, there are times when it seems that they will take anything *but* the flies that you are offering to them. This is generally when they are what is known as 'pre-occupied', which means that they have found that a certain kind of food is particularly plentiful in the water, and they will feed exclusively on that and ignore everything else. This makes it difficult for the fly fisher; unless the food on which the trout are feeding can be identified and imitated, the fishing will be very frustrating. Of course if the angler can find the right fly the fishing becomes very enjoyable indeed.

Trout feed at different depths and will search around their habitat for food, so you can be certain of seeing some fish at some time in the day's fishing if the water is well stocked.

Other fish are commonly fished for on the fly, while most fish will take a fly at some time. The brook trout is another fish from the United States which is sometimes stocked, and the grayling is a native but not very widespread fish which is fished for by fly. And there is of course the salmon, but this has now become a very expensive fish to fish for in most waters where it is common and where it is fished for by fly.

Brown trout

The brown trout is slower growing than the rainbow, but it can grow to larger sizes. This is because, being a native fish, it is better adapted to British waters and its lifespan is longer. It is a predatory fish which, when it reaches the larger sizes, may turn totally

Below: This insect, the blue-winged olive spinner, is comparatively easy for an angler to imitate with one of his own flies. The various kinds of olives provide food for trout and cause them to rise to dry flies.

Below: A trout rises lazily to take a fly. Allow plenty of time before striking with a slow rise like this.

cannibal and live on quite large fry (young) of other fish. It is usually stocked in sizes of only up to a pound (0·45 kg), because its slower rate of growth makes it a lot more expensive to grow in ponds than other trout. It can be found naturally in many rivers and streams throughout the United Kingdom and lives in Scottish lochs and Irish loughs as easily as it does in the lakes of England and Wales.

There are so many obstacles around that this fisher has had to wade into the trout stream to make his cast.

The still waters that the brown trout are naturally found in tend to be rather acid, and this means that the growth of trout in them is generally very limited. Small trout of about half a pound (0·23 kg) in weight are average, although the odd one that has turned cannibal grows very much larger. In the lowland lakes and reservoirs where brown trout are stocked on a regular basis, they grow quite rapidly. But the numbers of anglers on the water make them very wary, and to capture a large brown trout is quite a feat. As it grows older, the trout's feeding habits tend to become limited, and the larger fish live in deep water during the day and feed in the shallower water in the evening and early morning.

Sea trout

When brown trout are found in large numbers in coastal rivers, they often work their way out to sea and live there for a year or two. Then, like salmon, they return up their native river to spawn. They take on a much brighter silver colour than ordinary brown trout, and if they return to sea often enough they grow quite large and are great fighters when hooked on fly-fishing tackle.

Much sea-trout fishing is done at night. The fish are then more willing to take a fly than in the daytime, and their keen sight and awareness are

Two medium-sized sea trout caught in Loch Voshimid, in the Outer Hebrides of Scotland. The lower, larger fish seems to have been in fresh water longer, because it is slightly darker than the smaller one. Sea trout are silver when they first come in from the sea, and the longer they are in fresh water, the darker they become.

Fishing for sea trout from a boat in a highland loch.

Night fishing for sea trout. They are then more likely to take a fly than by day, and it is more easy to overcome their keen sight and awareness. Visit the place you hope to fish the day before, so that you can make a note of the likely places to find fish, and the possible difficulties. Test the bottom, if you are going to wade, and in particular make a note of any deep holes or places where you might trip. Make a note of any obstacles that might cause you trouble in casting. Taking care in advance will help you to get a good night's fishing.

A brace of fine trout – a brown trout (above) and a rainbow.

A good catch of grayling. These fish are dashing fighters, using their large dorsal fins to help them in a swift current. They like clear, fast water and cannot live in even slightly polluted streams.

This photograph shows very clearly the grayling's large dorsal fin and its graceful shape and colouring. You can see that it has larger scales than trout; it is also slimier and stronger smelling.

more easily overcome. The best conditions are fairly low water and warm, settled weather. During the day the fish live in sheltered, deep water, often under overhanging banks and rock ledges; they move to shallower areas after dusk.

Rainbow trout

The rainbow trout has become the most popular fish regularly fished for with fly – at least with the fish farmers. Rainbow trout grow very much faster than brown trout so it is possible to stock a water with quite large, or very large, rainbows in a short space of time. This is of course very attractive to most fly fishermen. In this way many fisheries compete for the custom of the fishermen, and there are even some small trout fisheries which stock with double-figure rainbow trout (of over 10 pounds, or 4·5 kg). In some of the larger reservoirs, rainbows will grow to considerable weights from stock fish of average size,

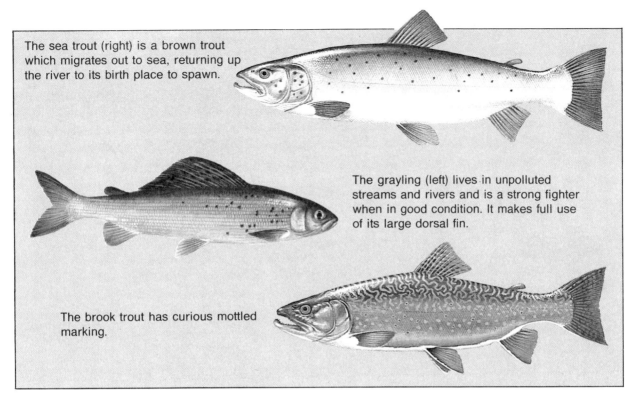

The sea trout (right) is a brown trout which migrates out to sea, returning up the river to its birth place to spawn.

The grayling (left) lives in unpolluted streams and rivers and is a strong fighter when in good condition. It makes full use of its large dorsal fin.

The brook trout has curious mottled marking.

Netting a trout stream to catch the grayling; these will be taken to new waters to provide sport for anglers, while the trout in the original stream have less competition for food.

but a double-figure rainbow from a reservoir is still a very rare fish.

Rainbow trout feed throughout the day, and even the larger fish will take a very small fly. They give very good sport and are powerful fighters, especially when they have been living in the water in which they are caught for a year or more.

The easiest way to tell the difference between rainbows and browns is that rainbows have spots on their fins and browns do not, while browns have spots on their gill covers whereas rainbows' gill covers are unspotted.

Brook trout and grayling

Not long ago, brook trout were introduced from the United States. Their unusual habits mean that they may be very easy to catch when they are first stocked into a water, but then they may disappear. It seems that many waters have now given up stocking them. They will not breed naturally in this country and so they have to be farmed. Because of this some fish farmers have attempted, quite successfully, to crossbreed them with rainbows and browns, and there are now some variations which have been given names like cheetah trout and tiger trout.

Grayling, unlike the other fish we have talked about, are not members of the salmon family, although, like trout, they have an adipose fin (see page 12). They are found most commonly in the rivers

Salmon

The salmon is sometimes called the 'king of the river'. It is bright silver when fresh in from the sea, growing darker the longer it stays in fresh water. On the left is a male (known as a cock) and below a female, or hen.

male

female

This salmon has been played into shallow water and can be 'handtailed' into shore without equipment. The salmon, alone among fish, has a 'wrist' to its tail before the tail fin starts, which makes it easy to grip by hand or with a noose called a tailer.

A salmon leaps clear of the water. These powerful fish make long and difficult journeys upstream to spawn in the rivers where they were born, often leaping up seemingly impassable rapids.

of southern England and Yorkshire. The grayling is a silver fish, plentiful in small sizes and less common as it grows larger; a 2-pound (1-kg) grayling is considered a large fish. Grayling feed on the same food as trout, and fishery owners generally look on them as pests in trout waters, removing them whenever possible. But they give good sport for fly fishers and if they are around they will rise to the fly on days when trout are reluctant to do so. They breed in spring, unlike trout.

The king of fishes

The magnificent salmon is the finest of all the game fish, but fly fishing for salmon is almost always very

Fishing for salmon in a fast-running stream. An estate worker waits beside the angler, to help him land his catch. Salmon can be heavy fish, and powerful fighters.

Salmon flies like these can be of all sizes and colours.

Every spring and summer, salmon leave the sea (1) to begin their remarkable journey back to their spawning grounds, braving rapids and falls as they fight their way upstream (2). At the breeding grounds they lay their eggs on the river bed (3). Tiny salmon hatch from the eggs (4), and when they are strong enough, after one to three years, they swim down to the sea as smolts (5). The adult salmon return to the sea after spawning. There are usually two major runs of salmon each year, one in spring and one in autumn.

expensive. (They can also be fished for with bait or by spinning.) Salmon fetch such a high price as food that they have been commercially fished on a large scale. They are netted in the estuaries as they return to fresh water to spawn, and some of the salmon feeding grounds at sea have been discovered and netted. As a result, there are now far fewer salmon about than there used to be.

Salmon need absolutely pure, unpolluted water in which to run and spawn. As a result they are found in some of the wildest and most beautiful country. They are great fighters, with strength and stamina, and specially strong rods and long lines are used in fishing for them. A 20-pound (9-kg) fish is a specimen. To the experienced angler, salmon fishing is the greatest sport of all, and it is no wonder that the fish is often called the 'king of the river'.

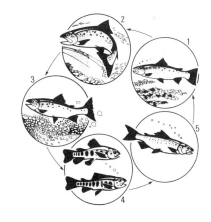

A short brook rod is used on a small stream, where trees and shrubs would make using a 10-foot (3-metre) rod extremely difficult. A short rod is also more accurate over short distances.

A typical still-water fly-fishing outfit. One rod has a floating line on it, and the other a sinking line. The bag is large enough to hold all tackle, the landing net, food and drink. On the bag is a priest, a weighted club used to kill the fish as soon as they are caught.

Tackle for Trout

When flyfishing first became a popular sport, the rods were made of greenheart wood and the lines were made of silk, greased to float and present flies at the surface. It was unheard of then to present a sunken line to the trout.

As time went by, rods were also made of cane and later of glass fibre; now some are made of carbon fibre. Meanwhile the lines and the methods of fly-fishing were going through drastic changes. Some anglers were actually causing their silk lines to sink, and so present a fly to trout lying deeper in the water – and were catching bigger fish. The lines then changed from silk to a plastic-coated fibre core. They were made in varying sizes and with different floating abilities and sinking rates. Then copper- and lead-cored sinking lines were introduced which sank very quickly indeed, and on the large and very deep reservoirs they are now in common use.

The most common materials used for rods these days are glass fibre (the cheapest) and carbon fibre (which can be the most expensive). To begin with a glass fibre rod would be the most suitable. Both rods and lines are numbered with what is known as a AFTM rating, from the Association of Fishing

Tackle Manufacturers. The rod and line numbers should match; using a line that has a lower number than the rod will mean that the rod will not 'work' properly because it is underloaded, while using a heavier line will overload the rod, which also interferes with casting. Fly-fishing rods vary in length from short brook rods of about 6 feet (1·8 m) in length up to 11 feet (3·3 m) for general use – salmon fly rods can be 16 feet (4·8 m) in length. To begin with a good average length for most waters is about 9 feet (2·7 m), with an AFTM rating of about 6.

Choosing a line

The choice of line is not only a matter of personal preference but also a matter of where and how you will be fishing. The basic choice is between sinking and floating lines but then you have to decide whether you would prefer a double-taper line to a weight-forward or a shooting head.

Double-taper lines have their thickest part, known as the belly, in the dead centre of the line, which is usually up to 33 yards (30 m) long, and it tapers at either end to its smallest diameter at the tip. It can be reversed on the reel when one end has worn out. Some people find that it is not the easiest line to cast with, but it does present the fly to the fish better than any other type of line.

The shooting head is basically half a double-taper line, or less, which has a light backing line attached to it. Once the head is in the air, the backing line can be released, and its light weight and slimness allow it to cast farther than the double-taper.

Weight-forward lines are a combination of shooting heads and double-tapers. The belly of the line is well forward of the middle part but it does not have the light backing, although the rear end of the line is plastic coated. This means that it does not tangle as readily as the backing on a shooting head sometimes does. Weight-forward lines may be cast farther than double-taper lines but do not present the fly as well.

Three materials for fly rods: carbon fibre (left), split cane (centre), and glass fibre (right).

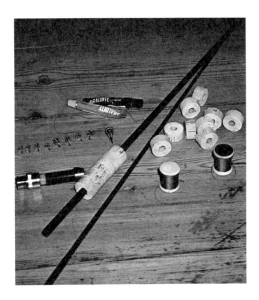

A rod-making kit ready for use; this can save you expense. The cork rings are glued to the blank and sandpapered to shape the handle.

This diagram (much condensed) shows the three types of fly line commonly used. In the double-taper line, the line tapers evenly at both ends; this means that you can wind it on to the reel from either end, which is economical. In the weight-forward line, the thickest part is nearer the front end; the shooting-head tapers at the front end only and is attached to a length of backing line.

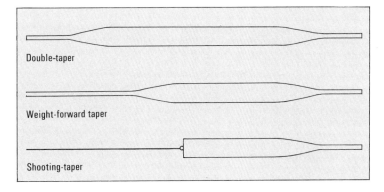

Double-taper

Weight-forward taper

Shooting-taper

Four types of fly reel. At the top left is an automatic reel (no handle is needed); at the top right is a carbon-fibre reel which has a large spool and is good for shooting-tapers as it prevents tangles in the backing. The multiplier (bottom left) turns the spool several times for each turn of the handle, while at the bottom right is a single-action reel.

Above right: Make sure that your landing net has a long handle, like this one.

Below: Cleaning your tackle carefully will give it longer life. Wipe the rod to clean it from grit, and wipe the reel with an oily rag. Drying is also important.

Reels, Hooks and Knots

The reel is not an essential part of fly fishing equipment as it is merely used to store the line – unless a very big or strong fish is hooked and rushes off 50 yards or more. When you are actually fishing, the spare line is laid on or in the water or it is laid at your feet if you are retrieving (drawing back) the fly. The fly is not retrieved by winding in the line as in spinning, for instance. There are reels which revolve the spool several times for each turn of the handle to make the winding in of line much easier, but there is really no need at all to spend a lot of money on a reel. The most basic one will do the job well, although a more expensive one may be better. There are now lightweight reels on the market which are worth thinking about. You hold the rod all the time that you are fly fishing and the less weight in your hand, the more efficient you will become as your tackle is better balanced.

The most important feature of the reel is the thickness of the spool's arbour or spindle on to which the line is wound. If it is very thin the fly line will wind on to it in tight coils, and when it is laid at your feet it will easily tangle. It may be possible to overcome this to a small degree by packing out the arbour before you put on the line (you will need some backing line anyway) and then the coils will not be so tight. The problem of line coils is greatest with shooting heads where nylon backing is used.

Straight-eye and wide-gape

Hooks are very much a matter of personal choice. There are a number of different designs in fly fishing and the design can be very important, because the hook is 'dressed' to catch the fish and the dressing may affect the hooking capabilities. The way in which the eye is set on the hook may also affect the way it fishes. If you are fishing with fairly light tackle you cannot use a lot of force to set the hook in the fish's mouth, so you should always match your hook to the tackle you are using.

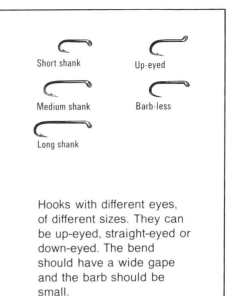

Hooks with different eyes, of different sizes. They can be up-eyed, straight-eyed or down-eyed. The bend should have a wide gape and the barb should be small.

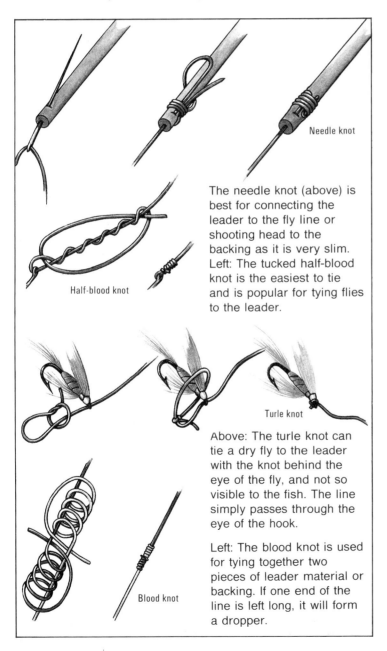

The needle knot (above) is best for connecting the leader to the fly line or shooting head to the backing as it is very slim. Left: The tucked half-blood knot is the easiest to tie and is popular for tying flies to the leader.

Above: The turle knot can tie a dry fly to the leader with the knot behind the eye of the fly, and not so visible to the fish. The line simply passes through the eye of the hook.

Left: The blood knot is used for tying together two pieces of leader material or backing. If one end of the line is left long, it will form a dropper.

You can see here the importance of a sound rod and tackle; this salmon rod is bent through 180° as a heavy fish is landed.

A selection of lures tied for fishing still water. All sorts of materials are used in tying flies.

Flies and How to Tie Them

In fly fishing there are basically two types of flies, wet or dry. A dry fly fishes on the surface of the water, and a wet fly fishes under the surface. These two types can be sub-divided into types of their own. Dry flies can be hackled (with a feather immediately behind the eye of the hook) or otherwise, up-winged or tied 'spent' which means with the wings flat-out. The wet flies can be subdivided into many more categories than the dry fly. There are traditional patterns which are winged or tied 'spider' fashion, nymphs, lures, streamers and a few others. The most important thing to bear in mind when choosing a wet fly is whether you want it to imitate a natural food or simply to attract. Flies known as attractors have not been tied to represent anything that swims in the water, but with flash or colour in them to attract the trout and trigger off its aggressive instincts.

Flies known as nymphs are usually tied to represent a hatching insect or some creature, such as a shrimp, that lives in the water and that the trout might expect to come across as food. Where the nymphs are fished in the water depends entirely on where the trout are feeding and the type of nymph that you are using at the time. They are usually fished slowly.

Lures are usually larger than most nymphs and dry flies. Some lures are tied with more than one hook. If they are tied on two hooks, one behind the other, they are known as 'tandem' lures; this is one way of creating a bulky fly without making it so heavy that it becomes difficult to cast. Most lures are attractors but some can be very imitative.

A typical wet fly (left), dry fly (right) and lure (below). The wings of the wet fly slope back over the hook shank and the throat hackle does not extend all round the shank. Dry flies can be tied with wings in many positions; the hackle almost always extends in a full circle. The much larger lure is more like a wet fly and is dressed to look bulky to the fish.

The natural daddy-long-legs (right) can induce some large fish to feed on the surface. This would be a good time to fish with the imitation daddy-long-legs (far right).

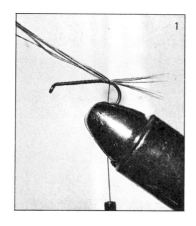
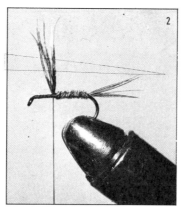

Tying a pheasant-tail nymph, a very simple fly to tie which can be produced in many varieties. First take a feather from the tail of a cock pheasant and strip from it the fibres you will need. Tie the thread to the hook and wind it back to the bend; tie in the tips of the pheasant fibres and leave them sticking out behind the hook (1). Wind the thread and fibres round the hook about two-thirds of the way towards the eye (2). Tie round some coloured wool, to form the thorax; snip off any left over and bring the thread back to the eye (3). Take the loose ends of the fibres, lay them over the thorax, and take several turns of the thread over them (4). Finish off the head and varnish it to make the finished fly (5). Many inventive fly-tiers create wonderful imitations of real insects and imaginary ones too. They use many different materials, including latex rubber.

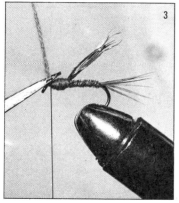
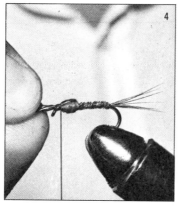

Below: A fly-tying outfit ready for use. On the right is the vise for holding the flies. A flexible type of lamp is particularly useful.

Below left: A realistic imitation of a prawn made from latex and seal fur. Prawns are often forbidden as bait for salmon.

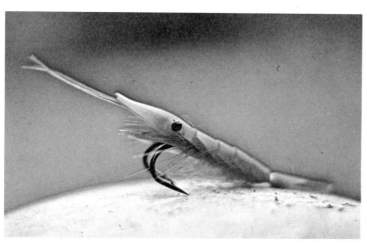

Casting a Fly

Casting; the single-handed grip shown here is most commonly used for trout.

Using a double-handed grip on a salmon rod.

On page 65 we mentioned the great importance of making sure that your rod and line are matched properly. If you do this then your casting will be very much easier. Possibly the easiest of all lines to learn to cast with is the weight-forward line, but a double-taper will stay in the air most easily of all if you are having problems because your forward or back cast is touching the water.

Four main stages
Basically there are four stages to fly casting. The **pick-up** or **lift-off** is the first stage, where the cast is about to begin.
The **back-cast** is the stage after the lift-off where the line is thrown behind.
The **forward-cast** is the opposite to the back-cast; the line is thrown forward of the rod.
The **delivery** happens when enough line has been extended and it is finally 'shot' on to the water, which 'delivers' the fly.

The principles involved in casting a fly are the same as casting a bait only in that the rod should be made to do the work for you. It should not be necessary to use a lot of force; if it is then your line is not matched to your rod. In fly casting for trout, usually only one hand holds the rod. Your 'spare' hand is used alternately to hold the line and to release line as it is required to lengthen during the cast.

Many beginners in fly-casting make the great mistake of trying to cast as far as possible. Fly fishing is *not* all about who can cast the farthest. If you present the fly well then you will catch fish, and trout can be caught under the rod tip in just the same way as coarse fish can. What is vitally important is to gain the correct rhythm and co-ordination, and then your casting will be good enough to catch fish regularly. Distance casting will improve with experience.

Casting off
To start the cast (assuming that you are right-handed) hold the rod parallel to the water with a length of line laid on the water ready for the lift-off. You will find that placing your left foot in front of your right will help. Hold the line firmly in your left hand, and lay enough line to complete the cast at

Stages in casting. The line is on the water; extra line is held in the left hand (1). The rod is taken back to 1 o'clock; the line streams out behind (2). The rod is brought forward to 10 o'clock and the line comes forward (3). The rod will begin to bend. On the next back-cast more line is let out (4); the rod bends more. The last of the line is let out as the line is brought forward again (5) before the tip is dropped to land the fly on the water (6). The actions are carried out briskly so that from start to finish casting will take much less than a minute.

your feet. Keeping your elbow tucked into your side, lift the rod smartly until it reaches a position behind your head that would be the same as '1' on a clock. Keep your wrist stiff, so that the rod does not fall behind you but is made to accept the load put on it by the line. And try to propel the line up at the sky rather than simply backwards. The line will travel out behind, and when it is extended behind the rod and you can feel it pulling against the rod, bring the rod forward smartly, keeping your wrist firm, so that the line is brought forward.

After the rod has stopped travelling – which should be at '10' on a clock – release line with your left hand and then stop it again, holding it so that the line extends forward of the rod without falling into the water. Do not release the line too early or it will stop pulling against the rod. This pull will also be released if you allow too much line through your left hand.

At all times you should be able to feel the line pulling against the rod and bending it rather like a spring. This is known as 'loading' the rod and it means that the rod is doing the casting for you.

When the forward-cast has extended and the rod is loaded as much as you feel it is going to be, repeat the back-cast, making sure that the line stays up in the air. By all means look over your right shoulder to make sure that the line is doing what you want it to. It should be flying back behind you in a loop which

This photograph shows how the rod is flexing as the rod is pushed forward with a straight wrist.

A roll cast is used in salmon fishing when obstacles on the bank make a proper back-cast impossible.

unrolls and extends. At this point start your forward-cast again. As the line unrolls on the forward-cast, release some more line, and while it still has momentum, stop it and again sharply start your back-cast.

When you have worked out enough line to complete the cast, you may 'deliver' the line. After releasing it finally with the left hand, as it extends over the water, lower the rod tip and allow the line to fall lightly.

Points to remember

There are a number of points to remember in fly-casting:

The line will always follow the path that the rod tip describes. If you move your rod tip around then the line will not be able to follow a straight path – and that is essential to make the rod work.

Keep your wrist as rigid as possible. If it is not rigid it will allow the rod to become 'lazy' and not do the work for you. It will allow the rod tip to move around, and it will also affect the accuracy of your cast.

By keeping your elbow in, you restrict the path of the rod, providing your wrist is firm, and this is essential for loading the rod.

The movement of the rod should not be greater than between 1 o'clock and 10 o'clock; this again is essential for the loading of the rod.

Do not release the line too early. This will cause the line to fall too soon and not form the loop it should, because the load will have been taken off the rod due to the release of line tension.

Keep your movement of the rod crisp, as in striking a nail with a hammer, and do not allow the rod to pull your wrist in any direction, other than where you want the rod to go. In order to achieve this, some fly fishers tuck the butt of the rod into the sleeve of their coat. This should not be necessary, but if you just try it you will see how the rod should behave.

Some rods have different action from others and if you try other rods you will see for yourself how important the timing of the back-cast and forward-cast is. A rod with a through action allows more time for the line to travel than a tip-action rod, because it is loaded all through.

As your casting improves, you may well develop a style that is different from the one we suggest here. By following the guide lines set out, you will acquire timing and rhythm. You will be able to find for yourself just what does suit you in the way of tackle and style once you are casting well.

Into the Net

Once trout are hooked they often put up a spectacular fight. It is not unusual for them to throw themselves well clear of the water, and very often they will make very fast and long 'runs'. Sometimes they thrash on the surface of the water and always they twist and turn in an effort to remove the hook. They are energetic fish, when they are in good condition, and will always provide a thrilling encounter.

Using your hands

As in coarse fishing, you should hold your rod high and keep pressure on the fish until it tires. But there is one very big difference between coarse and fly fishing. As we mentioned earlier, the reel is used only to store line and so you retrieve the line by hand.

After casting you should trap the line under the forefinger of the hand that is holding the rod, and then retrieve the line with the other hand. The finger that is trapping the line is used to hold the line as you strike your fish and hold it firm as you lift the rod. After that it plays the most important part of all. During the playing of the fish by hand the forefinger plays the part that a slipping clutch does on a fixed-spool reel (see page 27). If you hold the fish too hard your hook will tear out or the cast will break, but if you do not hold the line firmly enough the fish may come off because of slack line, or may be allowed to reach some obstacle or other. From there it may gain the upper hand and will probably be able to rid itself of the hook.

An angler plays a fish on a chalk stream in southern England.

A trout is brought safely into the net by a boat fisher. The angler is sensibly sitting with his centre of gravity well back in the boat to avoid accidents.

A good landing net is particularly important in a boat. With this short net the angler is slightly off balance, and if he had missed the fish it might have dashed under the boat.

If a fish runs off with all the slack line play it with the reel, letting the fish take line against the ratchet of the reel and winding in when the fish yields.

Fighting against the pull

Trout respond to being hooked in the same way as coarse fish – but they do it much more quickly than most coarse fish and they tend to be stronger, pound for pound. A trout will keep you on your toes from the instant that you set the hook to the moment that it is safely netted.

A brown trout usually fights much deeper in the water than a rainbow, and will perhaps not make such long runs. But it is a determined fish, and a characteristic of the brown trout is that it will get its head down and swim directly against the pull of the rod. Once it has got its head down the best way to alter its stance is to lay the rod hard over to one side and pull. This throws the fish off balance but it will try to repeat the performance of swimming directly against the pull, so you have to change the direction

If you are allowed to return a fish, do so as soon as possible after the moment you make up your mind to return it. If you see that you will be returning it while you are still playing it, then bring it in quickly and it will have some energy left for recovery when it goes back to the water.

The main stages in landing a trout. Keep the rod up as the fish is brought in (1). Get the head up (2), until the beaten fish is on the surface (3). Partly submerge your net (4) and draw the fish over it (5). (6) The happy angler displays a safely netted trout.

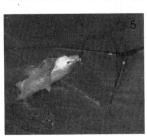

Farmoor reservoir provides very good fishing; a successful angler brings in a good catch.

If you can hold the fly, the fish may unhook itself without your handling it – a great advantage if you are going to return it (top). Artery forceps will help get out a stubborn hook (centre). Weighing the catch on a spring balance gives a measure of your success (bottom).

of the side strain. If a fish is off on a long run, just keep the rod up and bent towards it until it stops, and then try to recover line. Always be ready for it to start another run quickly; trout have tremendously fast reactions and you must not lose your concentration.

When a trout throws itself from the water, immediately release the pressure by lowering the rod tip and slackening the line until it is back in the water. If you keep the pressure on, it will snatch the hook free as it falls back into the water, or break the cast with the extra pressure – the fish weighs more in the air than in water.

If a trout comes to the surface and thrashes, do not keep the rod high as then the hook very often tears free. Lay the rod over and apply side strain; the fish will stop thrashing on the surface and go deeper every time. You can then come to terms with it more easily. Basically, the more changes of direction of pull you apply to a fish, the easier it will be to net.

Into the net
Once your fish has been played out it is ready to be netted. You must be able to lift its head up in the same way as coarse fishing. The line should be judged so that when the rod is at its highest point the fish will be over the waiting net. The net should be sunk in the water and the fish drawn forward. When the fish is over it, lift the net and release the pressure from the rod.

Most trout fisheries insist that you kill all that you catch and if that is the case, kill the fish with a sharp tap on the back of the head above the gill covers, using a priest (a weighted club). Do this before you unhook the fish so that it does not suffer from being out of the water.

Fishing a chalk stream for trout; these streams provide the best of all fishing, even though the fish caught may not be large.

Where to Go?

The most delightful of all places to fish for trout are the rivers and streams and lakes in which they are found naturally. There is nothing to better fishing with a fly in natural surroundings, even if the trout are only small. Such trout, small as they may be, can be difficult to catch and will give you much sport if you are using the right tackle.

Fishing for trout in streams and rivers can be limited, depending on where you live – and it can be much more expensive than coarse fishing. But in regions where trout are not found naturally, excellent trout fishing has been made possible for everyone by the stocking of trout into reservoirs, gravel pits and streams. In many instances completely new fisheries have been created by damming valleys or digging pools, and you can spend a day's fishing for a few pounds – or for quite a few pounds.

Three things to consider when you are making up your mind where to fish are the type of fly fishing you enjoy most; the cost; and the recent returns from a particular water, which will show if fishing there has been good.

76

A boat takes you right out over the deep waters of a reservoir, where you may catch a fine trout like this.

Playing a trout at Avington in Hampshire, where giant rainbows are stocked.

Small and large

Small fisheries created in the last few years are often stocked with rainbow trout that have been reared to a great size in a stock pond, sometimes reaching as much as 20 pounds (9 kg). They are often caught very quickly. These small fisheries tend to be the most expensive.

Large reservoirs are altogether different from any other fishery. They contain trout that feed at the surface and in the deep water, and conditions there vary very considerably. This is because wind can affect the trouts' feeding habits and some parts of a large reservoir can be very much more sheltered than others.

Keeping a record

Almost every trout fishery that stocks trout allows you to catch (and take home) up to a limited number of fish on a single ticket, and insists that the fish are killed upon capture. If they are returned to the water after a strong fight or after careless handing, they will probably sulk on the bottom of the water and die. Then the fishery owner will not know how many fish are in the water. All fisheries that are run as a business rely entirely on the anglers' catch records (known as returns) to let them know how many trout are in the water. If they did not know this they would either overstock or understock the water, which would eventually ruin the fishing and the fishery.

Trees

Weed

Current

Deep hole

Choosing your Method

The first thing to do when you arrive at the water you are going to fish is decide on the method of fishing you will use – dry fly, wet fly, or nymphing. The type of water you are fishing is obviously an important factor, but so too are conditions which vary from day to day, such as the weather and the state of the water.

The first thing to look for when you get to the water is rising fish. If the fish are rising, a floating line with a dry fly or a near-surface nymph is the obvious choice. If no fish are rising or showing, then a sinking fly – a wet fly or nymph – must be considered.

Sun or cloud?

Bright sunshine is usually a hindrance whatever method of fishing you use, but makes it especially difficult to fish near the surface in smooth water. As a rule, cloudy and dull weather is better for fishing at or near the surface, because then the shadow of the line is not so easily seen by the fish. Rain, on the other hand, can make dry fly fishing impossible, because the fly can be sunk again and again by raindrops.

Streams and rivers

Fishing in streams and rivers is governed very much indeed by the state of the water. Fish will tend to have different lies and feeding habits when the water

When fishing among foliage, the short rod is a definite advantage, making it less likely that your tackle will get tangled up among the foliage. The tackle needed for trout fishing is light and easy to carry, so it is a good idea to take a choice of rods with you.

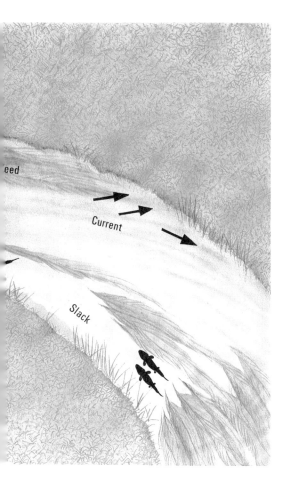

eed

Current

Slack

Where fish lie in typical stream conditions. They will be in places where there is plenty of food coming to them and where they can save energy – in deep holes, in and near weed beds, or in slack water, for instance. They may also be found lurking by overhanging trees, for the shade and for the insects dropping from the branches.

level is down from when it is high. They will also prove to be very difficult if the water is coloured (muddy) or very clear. Coloured water goes together with a high level and clear water goes together with low levels. The pace of the stream (current) will also have a bearing on how you are able to fish.

In general, if the level of the water is high and it is coloured, then the fishing will be difficult. The fact that the level has risen means that a lot of fresh water has been introduced into the river or stream and as a result the temperature of the river overall has probably been changed. Fish are susceptible to changes in temperature, and a sudden drop or increase in the temperature of their surroundings will stop them feeding for a time, or at least put them off. If the water is clear and low, on the other hand, they will be able to see much more of your tackle. The low level means that the current is slow and so the fish have much more time to inspect the fly and see if there is anything at all suspicious about it.

In running water, it is almost always preferable to use a floating line, whether fishing with a dry fly or a wet fly. It is rare to use a sinking line, unless the river is very wide or deep. The line will get snagged on boulders or weed. As it is easier to wade in rivers and streams (where it is permitted) light tackle is usually far better to use than the heavier tackle which is often seen on reservoirs.

Lakes and reservoirs
On natural lakes the accepted methods are dry fly or wet fly and these are fished with either a floating line or a slow sinking line.

The most difficult decision is the method to be used on the large reservoirs. The fish respond to all methods on these waters; you can choose one method and stick to it, only to find that it was a different method that caught fish at the end of the day. Sinking lines are often used on the reservoirs in England, particularly in the Midlands. The water is sometimes more than 100 feet (30 m) deep, and trout will live in very deep water and will not move into the shallows at all. A sinking line is essential for these. Fortunately, there are always trout at or near the surface and so it will be possible to catch fish with floating lines at any time, if that is how you prefer to fish.

The small man-made waters respond to very much the same methods as running water. They do not often have water that is more than 10 feet (3 m) deep and fish will come to a floating line on most days.

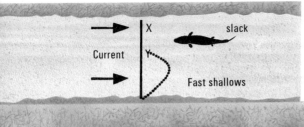

Dry Fly Fishing

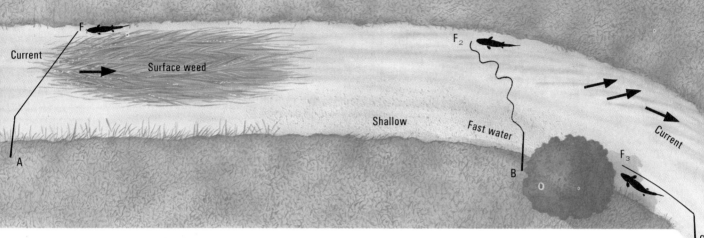

Top: If you cast straight across the stream, the fly will be dragged from X to Y by the fast water, alarming the fish.

Above: Where there is surface weed, cast cautiously straight from A to F₁. To avoid drag over fast water, cast a snaky line to F₂. To reach behind obstacles such as trees, cast from C to F₃.

Dry flies are designed to float on the surface of the water and entice fish feeding on floating insects. Dry fly fishing is the most enjoyable form of fly fishing, particularly in running water. It is not necessarily the most skilful way of fishing, but you are watching the fish and the fly together the whole time that anything is happening.

The art of dry fly fishing is to make sure that you place your fly in the correct place lightly, so that the fish does not realize that you are there. It is best to use the lightest possible leader, just in case you come across a difficult fish that has been in the river a long time. It will have seen many lines and flies and will soon know if anything is wrong with the fly.

The next step is to make sure that your fly will float

A selection of dry flies. The outline of the fly is the most important part of dry fly fishing. Whether it floats on the surface film or in it is also important and depends on how it is tied; a fly with a spun, bushy hackle will float much better than one tied in a lighter style. Trout feed on insects that live and die in the water, and on those that live on land such as ants, daddy-long-legs and bees which are found on the water by accident. Flies are tied to imitate all these. To be sure that your fly floats, dip it into a floatant and dry it before you use it. Then after each cast make a few false casts to dry the fly in the air.

over the fish naturally. It should land just above the fish and be floated down on the current. If you let the current pull the fly across, it will not look natural and the leader will make a wake on the surface. This is known as drag and is the worst that can happen to a dry fly. Sometimes a fish will take a dragged fly but older fish will be scared away from the area.

The right strike

Another very important part of dry fly fishing is the strike – the quick pull which sets the hook firmly in the fish's mouth. Remember that the fish has come from beneath the fly, and when it takes it its head will be inclined upwards.

If you strike then, you will pull the fly out of its mouth without hooking it. Wait until the fish has turned back down and then strike so that the hook will be set in a firm holding place. If the fish slashes at the fly you need not wait so long as if the rise is a lazy one, but you must pause every time you rise a fish. This means that you must concentrate on your fly the whole time that you are fishing it.

If you rise a fish that does not take your fly, try a smaller fly or one of the same shape but different in colour. The right combination could be easy to find, or hard; it will be enjoyable all the same.

Fishing a trout stream with a dry fly can produce the most exciting sport of all, as you watch the fish rise to take the fly.

'Dapping' on an Irish lough. In this type of fishing, either live or artificial flies such as mayflies or daddy-long-legs are allowed to be blown in front of the boat, as a wind-blown insect would be naturally. Specially made lightweight lines known as 'blow-lines' are used for this.

Inset: A cluster of mayflies on a branch.

Wet Fly Fishing

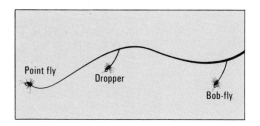

A cast of wet flies. The diagram on page 67 shows how a blood knot can be tied with one end left long for a dropper. The bob fly is the first to leave the water; fish which are attracted to it but do not take it may take one of the other flies instead.

Wet flies, as their name suggests, are fished beneath the surface. They can be fished with a floating line or a sinking line, depending on how deep you wish them to be. This of course depends on the size and depth of the water being fished. Still-water trout will take wet flies as easily as will trout that live in running water, and sometimes better.

Imitators and attractors

Wet flies fall into two main categories, imitators and attractors. The imitators represent drowned or hatching insects and the attractors have some bright colour on them which is intended to arouse the fish's aggression. Wet flies are moved through the water instead of being left to fish naturally like a dry fly. The speed and method of the retrieve of a wet fly can make a very real difference to whether it will catch fish or not.

Do make sure that you are allowed to fish with wet flies on the water of your choice; some rivers' rules absolutely forbid the use of wet flies.

The best way to fish wet flies is across the current, allowing the fly (or flies) to swing round, retrieving them when they are below you. A floating line is usually best for this, but if the water is deep or slow moving, a sinking line may be better. Fish very often take the fly as it has stopped moving across the current and is hanging below you. You may hear this referred to as 'on the dangle'. All trout will take a wet fly and it is the accepted method of fishing for sea trout. As this is often done at night, sea-trout fishing can be tremendously exciting.

Using several flies

The size of the wet flies can be very important and a cast of up to four flies is often used. This is done by the use of droppers from the main cast or leader. If

Step down the stream after every cast; this will cover all the water thoroughly and present flies to all the fish. Cast from A, B, C, D and E, and retrieve the line when the flies reach positions 1, 2, 3, 4 and 5 respectively. A fish may be covered more than once if you cast in this way.

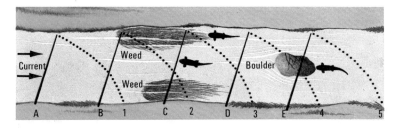

A selection of wet flies; these are rather larger than dry flies. Their wings are tied to slope back over the shank of the hook.

you do use more than one fly, the attractor should be at the end of the cast, or 'on the point' to give it the correct term. The top fly is the bob fly and any intermediate ones are droppers. The bob fly is the one that leaves the water first and it is a good idea to use one with a bushy hackle so that it creates a wake, particularly on still waters. On still waters it is usually the bob fly that catches more fish, because it is held at the surface as it is drawn slowly in so that it attracts fish from beneath. If they are attracted by the bob fly but fail to take it, they may take one of the other flies on the cast. The fish usually take the wet flies hard enough to hook themselves, but if the fish takes a bob fly at the surface, apply the same rules as dry fly fishing to the strike – pause until the fish has its head down again.

With wet fly fishing, because you are retrieving the fly, the fly line may cause a wake; it is best always to use as long a leader as you are able to manage.

Wading can be dangerous for you and disturbs the fish. Here the angler had to wade, the trees on both sides preventing him from fishing from the bank. Use a wading stick where possible to help you keep your balance.

Wading

The first rule about wading is only to do it when absolutely necessary, to get away from a bank where the backcast might get caught up or to avoid obstructions in the water such as boulders or rubbish. Wading stirs up silt on the bottom of the water, crushing insects on which fish feed and dislodging eggs before they are hatched. It makes fish aware that humans are around. For these reasons wading is forbidden in many waters. If wading is essential, it should be done on clean bottoms, quietly and with great care.

Nymphing

In nymph fishing you are always imitating a form of food that lives in the water (see page 68). Usually it is the early stages of insects such as mayflies, olives or midges that have laid eggs in the water. Other nymphs are creatures that live in the water all their life, such as the tiny freshwater shrimps. Nymph fishing is always done beneath the surface and can be just as effective with floating or sinking line, but a floating line is generally used.

It is important to find out just where in the water the trout are feeding on insects. Sometimes you will see a swirl on the surface; this means that the fish are feeding a foot or two beneath. Sometimes you will see the dorsal fin 'hump' lazily out of the water; then the fish are probably feeding on nymphs or insects trapped in the surface film.

A drifting fly

The golden rule in nymph fishing is to move your fly as slowly as you can. In running water do not move it at all. Most rivers and streams allow you to fish upstream only with nymphs, but this is the best way to fish them in any event.

When you have decided where your fish are feeding, cast the nymph with a floating line well upstream of the fish and make sure that your line and leader are in as straight a line as possible between you and the fly. The fly will drift down over the fish and if it is taken, the leader will dart forward. This is the time to strike firmly. If you are able to watch the fish this can be very exciting; but wait until it has closed its mouth on the fly before striking.

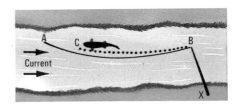

When you are fishing a nymph in running water you should normally retrieve the fly when it has passed the fish at B, but retrieving it at C might induce a take.

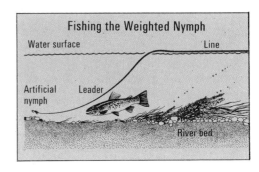

A weighted nymph trundled along the bottom will produce confident takes from trout feeding on the bottom. The line will dart forward when the fly is taken; just lift the rod to strike the fish.

Below: Large dark olive nymphs, part of the insect family of Ephemerids (short-lived flies), which are an important source of food for most species of freshwater fish.

Below left: This damsel-fly nymph also plays an important part in the diet of most fish.

Near the bottom

If there is no indication at all of where the fish are feeding, use a weighted fly with lead tied into the dressing. This will then fish nearer to or even on the bottom, which is a good place to catch the bigger fish that live in the waters. Pools are always a good place to fish a leaded nymph. Trout often hide beneath weeds and so if you see a clear path between weed beds, cast your fly so that it trundles along the bottom between the weeds. It is surprising how often a trout will dart from under a weed, take the nymph and disappear again. If this happens, strike and immediately maintain a firm pull downstream to get the fish out of the weeds; once it is out raise the rod and play the fish normally.

You may use more than one nymph on a cast, but this is practised on still waters more than anywhere. else. In running water you soon find out whether your fly is effective or not, and so one is enough. The leader should be as long as you can manage and as light as you can safely use.

The induced take

Sometimes a trout will inspect the fly as it passes and not take it. It may again show interest if you carry on using the same fly, and so you will have to try to induce it to take. Cast the fly upstream as before and allow it to drift down at the fish's level, or lower. As the fly approaches the fish's nose, lift the rod tip so that the fly comes up through the water just like an insect trying to escape. The fish will often forget about having a close look at the fly and instinctively snap at it.

Avoid a wake

Always make sure that your leader sinks when nymph fishing, unless you want the fly to stay very close to the surface. In still water, you can keep your fly close to the surface by greasing the leader, but you must be very careful of line wake. This means that you have to retrieve the fly very carefully or not at all. In still waters the leader will twitch when a fish takes the fly and it is safe to strike then. Often the fly line itself will move and you must be very quick to strike at this point or the fish will feel the drag of the line and spit out the fly.

Never hold the fly line too firmly when retrieving, because fish will often take the fly so hard that the leader will break if the line is not allowed to slip through your fingers. At the same time, do not hold it too limply or the hook will not set.

Fishing a nymph slowly on a still water, using a floating line.

Still Waters

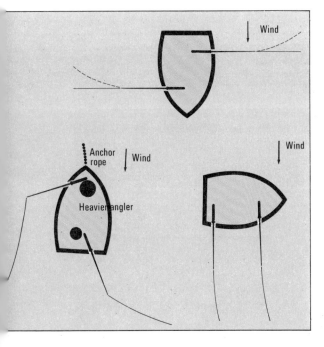

Fishing traditional-style on a Scottish loch, with the boat drifting broadside to the wind.

Fishing from a boat. When it is controlled from the stern (below), anglers should fish from either side. At anchor (below left) the anglers fish down and across wind. In short-lining, or loch-style fishing, the boat is controlled from the centre (below right).

There is really no such thing as still water in fly fishing. The water is always moving, because cold water sinks to the bottom of the lake or reservoir and the wind action creates waves which move the water. Wind and waves can actually create a strong current on still waters. Even so, the term 'still water' is commonly used for lakes and reservoirs.

Bank or boat?

On most still waters you have a choice as to whether you fish from the bank or from a boat. Which you prefer is a purely personal choice and the style or type of fishing can have a bearing on this. Dry fly fishing and nymph fishing are best from the bank, unless you are able to anchor a boat so that it does not swing with the wind changes. Obviously a boat is essential to find deep water over which to fish, unless the banks drop off very steeply. Sometimes bank fishing produces more than boat fishing but there are also times when the opposite is true. Boat fishing can be much more expensive because of the cost of maintaining and supervising the boats.

When fishing still waters, remember trout will almost always travel along the margins or up the wind. Because of this, you will cover more fish with nymphs and lures by fishing across the wind. It is often very effective to cast a team of nymphs across the wind on a floating line and to allow the wind to swing the flies around while you watch for takes. The fish move upwind to pick up food that is carried down by the wind, and so nymphs drifting naturally on the wind may be greedily accepted. Again it is really important that you find the correct depth at which to fish your flies.

Sometimes the wind has blown on to a bank long enough to stir up mud and you often see a long mud slick stretching into the reservoir against the wind. If you fish from that bank into the wind, the current will be strongest and going away from you. The food that drifts across the reservoir will also collect there or be carried out into the reservoir under the surface. This means that when bank fishing, it is safe to assume that there are always fish on the leeward bank (the bank that is 'downwind'; the 'upwind' bank is the windward bank).

A far cry from the nearly deserted loch; anglers fish for trout on Kempton reservoir. Over the past years, many such man-made waters have been stocked with trout, and as a result trout fishing, once mainly a sport for rich people, has become something everyone can enjoy.

Wind creates a current on still water. If the fish are not moving up wind, move down, casting as you go, from A to B and so on until you find the fish. Fishing from the point of a bank across the wind is a very good position. Fish moving up the wind pass close to the point and can be covered easily.

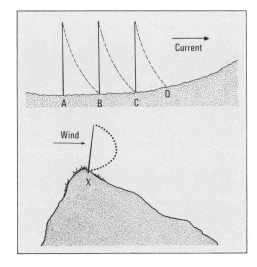

From dry fly to lure

Still waters are readily available to all fly fishers and all methods are effective on them, from the tiniest of dry flies to the largest of lures. They often contain big trout which have grown in the water, and the surroundings may be just as attractive as the loveliest of chalk streams. The problem with the larger waters is that you are rarely able to watch your fish, but it should be possible to apply the same methods to all types of trout fishing, whatever the water. For instance the trout in reservoirs do actually respond to the induced take, but you don't know most of the time that you are actually using it. Do not be afraid to experiment with flies and methods, and don't just do the same as every one else, especially if they are not catching!

Lure fishing

Fishing with the form of fly known as a lure is done almost exclusively on still waters. Lures are larger than other flies, sometimes with more than one hook and several centimetres long. They are not always intended to represent anything that lives in the water, except that they may look like small fish or leeches. They often have bright colours to attract the fishes' attention and arouse their aggression and the wings are often long and mobile, so that lures in general will have more movement to them than other flies. They are fished generally on sinking lines with a strong leader and can be fished at any speed. Often, when fish are preoccupied with some form of fly life that it is not possible or practical to imitate, a large lure retrieved fast will catch an odd fish. There may be little or no skill involved in lure fishing, but it can be as exacting as any other form of fishing.

In lure fishing it is more important than in any other form of fly fishing to fish at the correct depth. Unless a fish is feeding frantically it will not move far to take a lure and so the fly must be presented in front of its nose – and at the right speed. Lure fishing is most effective over deep water, and if the water is very deep then a lure fished on the bottom may be the most effective method of all. The early season and late season, when fish are feeding on small fry, are the best times to try a lure and the size of the effective fly will depend on the temperature of the water. If the water is cool, a smaller fly will be most successful and if the water is warmer the fish will take a larger fly.

Colour selection

Generally the rule with lures is that on bright sunny days, a brightly coloured fly will be most effective. But this is not necessarily so. On some occasions the trout will not take a lure that does not have a bright colour in it, but the weather may not have anything to do with it. Whatever the weather, try all colours at all depths and at all speeds of retrieve. If you use a bright fly, it will often have to be retrieved fast. The main colours used in lures are white, black, yellow and orange. A lure can be just one colour or a combination; the selection available is enormous, particularly when size is also considered.

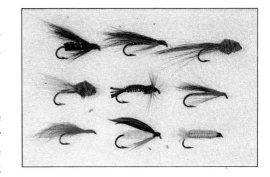

A selection of lures for use on large still waters.

Wake flies, as their name suggests, are fished on the surface of the water to create a wake, which attracts fish to them. They are most successful in dull conditions.

Do not forget – when you are sorting through a fly box you cannot catch fish. Find a few general patterns that you are happy with and these should be enough to catch fish on all occasions.

Coarse Fishing with Flies

A superb pike taken from a trout reservoir on a large lure. Its diet of trout helped it grow to such a size.

A zander, or pike-perch, taken on a fly. When hooked it will usually fight very well.

A specimen bream taken from a still water on a lure.

Everyone who fly fishes often will have caught coarse fish by accident at one time or another. I have caught, on lures, specimen roach, bream and perch and I have also caught a good number of smaller perch and some pike. Generally it is the predatory fish such as perch and pike that will take a fly, and it is also these fish that accidentally occur in still waters that contain trout. They feed on the same sort of food as trout (as well as on the trout themselves) so it is reasonable to expect to be able to catch them on the same sort of flies. Some very big pike have been caught on flies, but usually they bite through the leader and get away if they are of any size. Pike appear to respond better to yellow and white lures, whereas perch will take most colours. It is better to move the lure slowly to catch coarse fish.

Other fish that can be caught on fly are chub and zander. The zander responds to the same sort of fly as pike but the chub will take nymphs and dry flies.

Cunning chub

Chub fishing with flies can be great fun. They react to a dry fly in very much the same way that you would expect a trout to. They are also very cunning fish and will disappear slowly from view if they suspect that all is not well. Being partly predators they will also take a lure. Any size of fly will be considered by a chub. It has a large mouth, but does not take anything that it cannot devour in one go, so your fly should be geared to that. On the other hand, pike and zander will take a bait that is larger than they can handle with one mouthful and so a large fly is better for them.

You will not often see people fly fishing for coarse fish, but that should not put you off trying it. Once when the trout season (see page 112) was closed, I was asked to try a new fly rod and so I decided to try to catch some pike on it with lures. Using a yellow lure on a very cold December's day, I caught three pike on a fly and my partner, using a spinner, caught nothing.

This ballan wrasse was caught from the rocks. They provide exciting fishing but can be dangerous. Never scramble over rocks and cliffs by yourself.

A catch of small mackerel, taken on feathers on a multi-hooked rig from a boat.

Sea Fishing

Britain is a collection of islands, so there is plenty of sea fishing for everyone who lives there. Most of it is excellent and it is very varied. For some people it may mean quite a long day out because they are not very near to the sea, but everyone in Britain can reach the sea by car or train within a few hours.

Boat fishing

Boat fishing is a very good introduction to sea fishing itself and there must be many anglers whose first taste of fishing at sea was mackerel fishing on a holiday. When boat fishing you can fish in an estuary and be close to the land, or you can be a very long way out to sea with no land in sight at all. For this reason it is essential that you join an experienced party with an experienced skipper handling the boat. The reason for travelling such long distances out to sea is to reach features which attract fish; sometimes these are sandbanks or areas of rocky seabed, but often the very experienced skippers discover wrecks of ships which attract fish.

Feet on the ground

If you would rather keep your feet on dry land, there is still much scope for you on the beaches and at places such as harbours which attract fish. Some quite big fish can even be caught from the beach or harbour wall. The fish that come close inland are usually flatfish such as dabs and plaice. The cod comes close inland at some times of the year and it is usually possible to catch dogfish and other scavengers. The bass is a keenly sought fish in many parts of the country and a specimen mullet from a harbour is a feather in anyone's cap. The fishing varies a great deal from one part of the coastline to another and local knowledge is very important.

No great outlay

Although you may wish to take up sea fishing seriously, it may not be necessary to spend a lot of money on new tackle. If you are just going to catch the odd smallish sea fish from a harbour wall, pier or jetty, the sort of tackle that you use for heavier coarse fish could be used. If you are going to try to cast long distances or use heavy leads, then it would be better to look carefully into the sort of tackle that you will need. There are some excellent sea fishing rods and reels available which do not cost a great deal of money.

A pair of red bream, which are summer visitors to the southern coasts of Britain. Most bream are caught from boats.

Harbours provide good fishing, as fish feed on refuse and among weeds. These boys are fishing from a breakwater.

Types of Fish

The range of fish species in the ocean is so enormous that it is not possible to give more than a brief account of the ones that you are more likely to encounter. It would need a complete book to mention them all.

Mackerel are a common fish, although in recent years very heavy and efficient industrial fishing has reduced their numbers drastically. They can be caught from shore and from boats. The usual method is to troll feathers or spinners from a drifting or moving boat, but they can also be caught by spinning or float fishing from a pier or jetty. The baits used most often are strips of mackerel skin and flesh.

Flounders are found all round the British Isles and are easily caught from the shore. They are flatfish which do not grow large, and they prefer muddy-bottomed waters. The best baits for flounders are razorfish cockles, lugworm and ragworm.

Bass are the favourite fish of many sea anglers. They are found mainly around the southerly parts of England, Wales and Ireland. Although they often move into estuaries they are mainly sought by rock and surf fishermen. They are slow-growing fish and most anglers now return immature bass to the water.

A good catch of plaice, the most familiar flatfish. Plaice are easily identified by their orange spots.

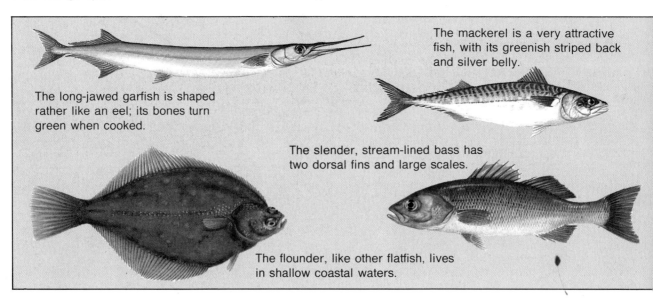

The long-jawed garfish is shaped rather like an eel; its bones turn green when cooked.

The mackerel is a very attractive fish, with its greenish striped back and silver belly.

The slender, stream-lined bass has two dorsal fins and large scales.

The flounder, like other flatfish, lives in shallow coastal waters.

The usual baits are live sandeels and prawns, peeler and soft crabs, ragworm, lugworm and strips of fish or squid.

Cod tend to show up around the entire British coast, mainly in the autumn and winter. They grow quite large and, of course, are highly thought of as food. Beach fishermen spend many hours trying to catch specimen cod but they can also be taken from quieter places such as harbours. The larger cod are caught by boat anglers. Baits used are very much the same as for bass.

Dogfish often take baits intended for other fish and so are not held in high regard by the average sea angler. There are several dogfish species; the ones that you will come across are the lesser spotted, the greater spotted and the spur (which has a venomous dorsal fin). They look like a small shark and will take virtually any bait that is offered, but prefer fish and crabs.

Pollack resemble cod in shape and grow to quite a large size. They live in deep rocky areas but can also be caught around harbours. Again they prefer fish baits, but also will take peeler crab and lugworm and ragworm.

Grey mullet are a very wary species of fish found mainly in brackish water, harbours and estuaries. They may be caught on light float tackle and tiny baits are essential. The baits used are bread flake, tiny harbour ragworms and small pieces of mackerel flesh. Pieces of bacon fat have been successful.

A catch of mullet. These are usually caught on freshwater tackle with groundbait of tiny pieces of bread or fish.

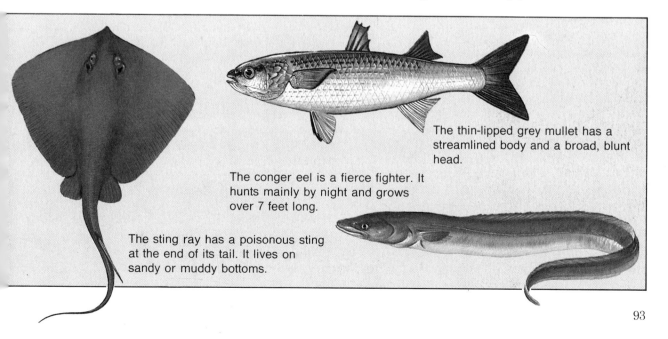

The thin-lipped grey mullet has a streamlined body and a broad, blunt head.

The conger eel is a fierce fighter. It hunts mainly by night and grows over 7 feet long.

The sting ray has a poisonous sting at the end of its tail. It lives on sandy or muddy bottoms.

This picture of a conger eel shows its mouth; its sharp teeth and strong jaws can bite very hard. Conger live among rocks and in sunken ships; the biggest are found off the south-west coast of Britain. They are great fighters and can only be caught on strong tackle with a wire trace – they easily bite through any other material.

Plaice are found all round the British Isles, also in estuaries. They seem to prefer sandy areas to the muddy type of bottom that the flounder likes. They live on shellfish, such as mussels and cockles, which are a successful bait, and the more popular bait like ragworm and lugworm also work very well.

Wrasse are another common fish caught all round the British Isles. There are two species, the ballan wrasse and the cuckoo wrasse. The cuckoo is more brightly coloured and is not as common as the ballan; nor does it grow as big. Wrasse live in deeper water and prefer clean bottoms and rocky areas; weed beds are also an attraction. They are to be found closer to the shore in summer and autumn and the usual baits such as rag- and lugworms and peeler crabs work very well.

Tope are members of the shark family and are fished for by many anglers. They do not grow as large as most shark species but on the right tackle they will fight hard. They swim close to the bottom and prey on other bottom fish. Their teeth and rough skin make a wire trace essential, although a heavy line is' not especially necessary. They can be caught from the shore, but more often are caught when boat fishing. Other fish such as mackerel and herring are used for bait, either whole or filleted.

Conger eels are large and dangerous creatures which must be treated with care and respect. They grow to large sizes and can bite through a sea boot if they are given the opportunity. Only experienced anglers should try to cope with them. They live around piers and harbours as well as sunken wrecks and are always to be found near the bottom, usually within easy reach of some obstacle or hiding place. Their favourite tactic when hooked is to wrap their tail around some obstacle, from which it will be extremely hard to move them. Heavy tackle and large fish baits are needed for conger.

Garfish are a sporting little fish, rather like a miniature swordfish in shape. They are caught by accident, usually when fishing for mackerel. They take a spinner fished near the surface and leap into the air when hooked. Their bones turn green when they are cooked.

Black bream and **red bream** are found mainly around the southern and western coasts of the British Isles, usually in rocky areas. They do not grow very large and are caught mainly by boat anglers. Smaller bream are found nearer to shore. They are caught on lug- and ragworm, mussels, limpets and strips of other fish.

Shark need no introduction. They are sought by many anglers from boats. The main species which are caught are blue shark and porbeagle. The porbeagle grows larger than the blue. Heavy tackle is very necessary and plenty of line must be on the reel. Other fish are used as baits and great care must be exercised when a shark is in the boat. The skin is rough like glass paper, and will graze the bare human skin very easily.

Rays are a flatfish with a difference. They can be quite large and they all have a tail. The sting ray has a sting in its tail. Most of them have a distinguishing feature by which they are known, such as the sting ray, the thornback ray, the small-eyed ray and so on. They are found all round the British Isles, mainly in clean areas, and the baits generally used are strips of mackerel or herring or whole sprats or peeler crab.

You will catch other fish such as pouting and whiting and turbot, so if you are doing a lot of sea fishing, you will find it very useful to have a good reference book in which you can look up all types of sea fish.

A specimen tope, caught off the Isle of Wight. This graceful member of the shark family hunts in sandy bays in summer, moving out to deeper water in cold weather. Like others in its family, it is a great fighter.

This angler has every right to look proud of his catch – a record-breaking bass of over 11 pounds.

Playing a large fish from a boat. The angler wears a harness, which gives leverage against the strength of the fish, and is using a very strong rod and big-game reel.

Spoons and spinners used in fishing different species of sea fish.

SeaTackle

As we have already mentioned, it is possible to start sea fishing with some coarse-fishing tackle, such as spinning gear or carp or pike tackle. The main point to remember is that sea water is very corrosive, and if your tackle is not of a good standard it will rust easily and you will ruin a set of tackle. Wash all tackle in fresh water as soon as you get'home, then dry it. Oil all metal objects. The sea-fishing rods and reels that are designed for the purpose are all specially finished to prevent them from rusting if cared for properly.

Rods for beach or boat

Boat rods and beach rods vary enormously. A boat rod is not designed to cast long distances and so is short and stubby, sometimes with a roller built into the tip ring. This is for lifting heavy fish where an ordinary tip ring might break or cause the line to break. Boat rods also need to be thick because they are used in conjunction with heavy sea leads to combat the strong tides and deep waters that are fished.

Beach casters are longer rods altogether but are no less powerful than a boat rod. They need to cast a fairly heavy lead a very long way and so they are designed to have a lot of spring in them to catapult the lead and tackle as far as possible. The most common material is glass fibre although a few beach casters are carbon fibre; these are very expensive but glass fibre can be relatively cheap.

You will also need a large collection of other tackle. A drop-net is very useful when you hook a fish that is too large to be hauled up by hand from high above the water. It is simply a metal hoop with netting attached to it that you lower into the water on a cord, encouraging the fish over it until you can lift it from the water.

Leads come in various shapes and sizes and the shape and weight needed depend on what you are fishing for and from where. Shore-fishing leads are normally more streamlined than boat-fishing ones because they need to offer less resistance to the air to reach greater distances. Floats are large and buoyant and sliding floats are better for deep water fishing; paternosters are a method of keeping your actual hook just off the bottom so that snags are avoided (see page 101).

For ordinary pier or harbour wall fishing, a fairly powerful rod of any sort will do. But you must remember that there is always the possibility of hooking a powerful fish. Fishing heavy all the time, however, may well mean that you catch fewer fish anyway, and so you must really try to strike a happy medium. As with other fishing, try to match your tackle to the sort of fishing that you will be doing.

Reels, nets and leads

Reels will cost you more than a coarse-fishing reel. You can choose either a multiplier or a fixed spool. The most effective reel for sea fishing is a multiplying reel but it can be difficult to start with. A fixed-spool reel can be just as good. The main requirement of a sea reel is that it must be able to hold a good deal of line.

A collection of sea rods; glass fibre is by far the most common material for these. All these rods are powerful, and fitted with multiplier reels.

A collection of leads and floats used for sea fishing. These leads are much heavier than those used for freshwater fishing, and it is important to be very careful when you are casting with them.

Sea Bait

The bait that you use depends, of course, on the fish that you are hoping to catch. Sometimes that bait may be easy to find and sometimes it may be hard. When other fish such as mackerel or herring or whitebait are to be used as baits it may be possible to use deep-frozen freshly caught fish. Most anglers prefer to use freshly caught fish as bait and this is certainly best, but not always possible.

Sandeels are a very popular bait for species such as bass and cod as well as many others. They may be used alive or, more commonly, dead.

Ragworms are another very popular bait and will catch almost any species of sea fish. The king ragworm is capable of giving a nasty nip to the fingers.

Lugworms again will catch almost any species of fish and are fairly easy to get hold of.

Peeler crabs are crabs about to shed the old, dead shell, under which they are soft and rubbery. They are called soft crabs when they have shed the old shell and before the new one hardens. They make excellent baits for bass, cod and many other bottom-feeding species.

Sandeels make good bait, particularly for bass and cod. They are hard to keep alive, so are more usually fished as deadbait.

Baiting a hook with a king ragworm, which is a good bait and particularly effective for bass. Most sea fish are not fussy feeders, but it is best to ask locally what baits are successful.

Lugworms look much like earthworms and live in the mud and sand along the shore. They are the most widely used bait for sea fishing. These are kept alive on damp newspaper.

Fresh mackerel, cut into strips, makes a good bait for the larger fish, particularly those which hunt partly by smell.

A peeler crab makes a very good bait for most sea fish. The name 'peeler' is given to a crab of several species which is just shedding its hard shell, as you can see this one doing.

Squid is used by many anglers for all sorts of fish. It is a very good bait for cod, bass and conger among others.

Shellfish are quite easy to obtain and make excellent baits for many fish. The main sorts of shellfish used are mussels, cockles, razorfish, slipper-limpets and limpets. Of course, they are removed from their shell and used on the hook without their usual protection.

Sprats and **whitebait** are used dead for species such as bass, cod, whiting and dogfish.

Mackerel and **herring** are used for the larger fish such as tope, shark and conger. If the bait need not be as large as a whole fish, it can be cut into strips or fillets. This also has the effect of giving some movement to the bait and releasing the natural oils of the fish into the water, which attracts those fish that hunt partly by smell.

Prawns and **shrimps** are used alive on float tackle and hooked through the tail for bass and pollack.

Spoons and **pirks** are used very often for some fish. Many cod are caught on pirks; these are heavy metal faceted lures which are lowered to the sea bed and either left to flutter in the tide or 'jigged' up and down to give them action. Spoons can be of varying sizes and weights and are sometimes baited to give them added attraction.

Feathers are used mainly for mackerel fishing and are cast and retrieved in the same way as a spinner. Large feathers are used for cod, pollack and coalfish.

Harbours and Piers

Piers and harbours are very popular with children and adults alike and are the safest of all places to fish in the sea – when treated with respect. Many species of fish congregate around them because they attract the sort of food that many sea fish like, providing a kind of larder. Shellfish, crabs and small fish collect around the legs of piers and jetties, and amongst the weeds. Quite a lot of rubbish is thrown away in harbours and this also attracts fish.

Fishing from a height

Another popular feature of piers and harbours – as far as anglers are concerned – is that getting there is no problem. It is normally possible to leave your transport near to the fishing spot and simply walk a short distance to where you want to fish.

If you are fishing from well above the water you will need a stiff rod – not rigid but stiff enough to haul fish quite a way from the sea up to where you are. If the fish is too big for this you will need a drop net (see page 97).

Float fishing, legering and spinning are the main methods of fishing from piers and harbours. It is better to use a sliding float when float fishing; you will be fishing quite a depth of water and if you want

Docks, like harbours, provide food and shelter for fish, and workers may well be lucky in a few minutes' fishing during a break.

Rough blocks of concrete at the harbour mouth provide good fishing; scraps of food and other rubbish thrown into harbour waters attract many fish.

the bait to be well down the float must be set at a greater depth than the length of the rod. To use a fixed float would be impossible. Instead the line is passed through a hole in the float and a bead or other form of stop is fixed on the line a long way from the hook and bait. When the tackle is cast out the line slides through the float until it reaches the stop, and the float then is able to work as well as if it were fixed in the first place. When legering, a running leger or a paternoster rig may be used.

No need to cast
All the usual sorts of bait including spinners and feathers can be fished from piers, and many species of fish can be caught. It is not often necessary to cast a long way because the legs of the structure will attract food for the fish, and so it is often possible just to lower the tackle over the pier. If you use a lead that is not quite heavy enough to hold the bottom against a tide, you will be able to stream your tackle out and so cover more water. In harbours, the water is quieter and more sheltered. The fish swim at varying depths but there will always be some form of flatfish to be found and sometimes some specimen mullet to tax your patience and intelligence. Harbour-fishing tackle need not be heavy because you can usually get down to the water by steps or ladders if a heavy fish is proving a difficulty.

Fishing from the angling deck of Deal pier. The legs of piers under water attract shellfish and small fish, acting as a 'larder' for larger fish. A line suspended close to the pier legs is likely to be successful.

A paternoster rig has a large lead at the bottom, with two or three hooks on nylon droppers or on wire or plastic arms above it. This rig keeps the baits from getting tangled up in the main line, and is used in coarse fishing as well as sea fishing.

Casting

This angler is beginning his beach cast. Make sure before you start that there is no one close to you; heavy leads can deal a nasty blow.

Whether you are casting from a beach or from a pier, you should exercise great caution for the sake of your own safety and that of others nearby. The leads that are used weigh from 2 to 6 ounces (57 to 170 g) so that they will travel greater distances. If one of these leads is sent in the wrong direction by a poor casting action it can cause serious damage.

The rods that are used for casting are normally powerful, otherwise they would not be able to handle the heavy leads. Only practice will improve your casting, but there are some basic principles to remember for accurate and good casting.

Into action

The main method used by most people is the layback method. You should stand with your left foot forward, if you are right handed. This means that you will be at a slight angle to the sea. Your right hand should be near to the point of balance of the rod while the lead and bait are hanging, and your left hand should be near to the butt of the rod. Bring the rod back round your right shoulder and put your weight on the right foot. Smoothly bring the rod forward, with your right hand starting to push upwards to flex the rod and your left hand pulling down. As your body swings round your weight should be transferring to your left foot until all the

Another beach angler at the end of his cast; his weight is now firmly on the front foot. Both his tackle and his style look rather old-fashioned!

Shoals of cod come close to shore in the winter months. This fine pair was caught from the beach at Folkestone; the biggest fish are caught from boats.

weight is on that foot. At the completion of the cast you will be leaning forward with the left hand pulled into your body and your right arm extended. As in coarse fishing, the line is held by your right hand until it is time to release it. This should be after the lead has passed the tip of the rod and is in motion through the air.

Controlling your line

Generally multiplying reels cast farther and retrieve line quicker but it is possible to fish adequately with a fixed spool. If you do use a multiplying reel, make sure that you stop the line running from the spool the instant that the lead hits the sea. If you fail to do so you will cause a terrible tangle on the reel. Whatever type of reel you use, stop the free running as soon as possible after completion of the cast, unless there is some good reason not to do so. Such a reason would be if you were spinning and wanted the spinner to sink deep before retrieving.

If you stop your line going out straight away, the sinking of the lead should mean that you will have a tight line to the bait, when bottom fishing. This in turn means that bites will be easier to detect. Your rod should be put into its rest as soon as possible. Of course if you are float fishing this is not so important, because you are able to see what exactly is happening by the action of the float.

If you intend to cast long distances, make sure that you have a fairly long rod and one with tip action. This will help your casting greatly and improve your enjoyment of fishing from the shore.

On the Rocks

There are many parts of our coastline that are spectacular to look at and especially pleasant to be around. In these areas the sea does tend to be rather more rough at times than you will find it in other aspects of sea fishing. If you are intending to fish from rocks and cliffs, you should arrange for a party of anglers to fish together in case of accidents.

In search of food
The advantage of rock fishing is that bass and other sporting fish move in with the tide looking for the food that the high tides will cover. The sort of food that they will be seeking will be crabs, prawns, sandeels and small fish. Some of these can be obtained as bait by looking in the rock pools that are left behind at low tide.

Fishing for bass on sandy patches among the rocks. This is good sport but can be dangerous; never go alone and remember that wet rocks get very slippery.

Landing problems

When trying to land your fish from rocks, use the incoming waves to help you if a fairly heavy sea is running. But do not try to pump a fish in against outgoing waves or you will probably lose it; the waves will try to pull it back again and the fish will use their help in getting away.

A drop net, landing net or gaff may be used when you are fishing from rocks and cliffs, depending on how close to the water you are fishing. A gaff is a sharp hooked instrument which is used to hook a beaten fish at the point of balance and heave it ashore. It should only be used when a fish is too large for a net. A flying gaff is one that is attached to a length of rope because a handle would not be long enough to reach the fish.

Float fishing is a very popular method from rocks and cliffs when the water is reasonably calm. Legering and paternostering are also very effective, with the usual baits. Spinning is another method that is practised often from rocks. Bass and mackerel particularly are species of fish that come in close near rocky areas and both of these will attack a spinner that is fished properly.

Fishing Matches

A fishing match in progress. This sort of competition is very popular, particularly for coarse fish.

All fishing is a competitive sport – we are pitting our wits against those of the fish. We also like to catch bigger and better fish than other people, and matches and competitions are a regular feature of all forms of fishing.

Coarse fishing has more competitions than fly or sea fishing. Canals and rivers are the most popular venues for these events and there will be an event somewhere in your area, or within easy reach, every weekend of the fishing season. The larger clubs all arrange coach transport so that their members can attend.

Match rules
In most matches you may not fish just where you choose to. At the beginning of the day you are given a starting time and a finishing time, and then peg numbers are drawn for everybody taking part in the event. A peg is the stretch of water that you are allotted to fish, and you may not move from this peg to fish elsewhere after the whistle has gone. The whistle is used to start the match and to end it. All the fish that are caught are kept in a keep net. Fishing must cease immediately the final whistle has been

Elastic is used as a shock absorber to play a fish on a roach-pole because of the absence of a reel. With a pole it is possible to keep the float and tackle in exactly the same spot for every cast.

The proud winner of a trout fishing competition with his catch. As in coarse fishing matches, the total weight is what counts, not the number of individual fish.

Competitors in a junior match watch as their catches are weighed at the end of the day.

blown, and then officials move down the line from one competitor to the next, weighing the fish on very accurate scales. The winner of the event is the angler who has caught the heaviest bag of fish – not the one with the greatest number.

The catches vary greatly in weight and types of fish depending on where the event is held. Some matches on rivers may be won by a very heavy bag of fish such as bream and chub, but the events held on canals are usually won by a lot of smaller fish. Your chances in any match depend a good deal on the peg number that you draw at the start of the day.

Junior matches are arranged by many clubs and quite often these are fished as 'rovers'. This means that you may search the water, within the confines of the club limits, throughout the day. This will improve your chances of catching some better fish.

Wily competitors

It is possible to win a lot of money at large events and so anglers will go to great lengths to improve their chances. They fish with very light breaking-strain lines and use many different kinds of baits. Long roach poles have recently come into use (see page 27). The French are especially clever at the efficient and speedy use of these poles. No reels are used, and either the fish is swung in if it is small enough, or the pole is reduced in length by taking off sections or by pulling it in hand over hand until the fish is near enough to net.

Safety and Conservation

When we talk about safety and conservation we are referring to our own safety and the conservation of our sport by the considerate treatment of fish. Obviously personal safety is something that is very important to all of us – but it is also important to our families and friends. No matter how competent we may be, accidents do happen. When we are fishing we become engrossed in the sport and very often we overlook the possible hazards that we meet. These may only be small things such as breaking some part of your tackle, but major risks include the loss of an eye – or worse. Read and obey any warning notices and make sure you obey all rules.

Care in casting

Always consider the conditions when you are fishing and make sure that what you intend to do will be safe. This is particularly important where tackle is propelled through the air at speed, as in beach casting and fly fishing. Make sure there is no one close to you. In fly fishing be careful of the wind

This boy is sensibly wearing a lifejacket to fish from a boat over deep water. He has resisted the temptation to lean over the edge of the boat as he brings in his catch. Always take care when you are fishing; the excitement of catching a fish makes it easy to forget basic rules of safety but accidents can easily happen.

which can blow the fly into your face; it is a good idea to wear sunglasses to protect your eyes. If you are fly fishing for coarse fish, remember that people around you may not be as aware of the dangers of back-casts as they would be at a trout fishery, and make especially sure that there is no one close behind you.

Sea fishing is altogether more disastrous if the sea is not treated with caution and respect. It is essential that you do not take any risks and that you do not fish alone from somewhere where you would get into difficulties if you should fall in. Rocks and wet surfaces are particularly slippery. Above all, be careful of incoming tides. Always make sure that your family know where it is that you are going to be; this will save them from worry.

Fish for the future

Conservation is of the greatest importance in these times of pressure on all forms of fishing, so return your fish to the water in good condition. The only exception is on the 'put and take' trout fisheries where rules state that all fish must be killed.

Always handle fish to be returned with care. Remember that it is uncomfortable for fish to be out of the water and return them as quickly as possible. Handle fish being returned with wet hands and do not handle them so roughly that their scales are knocked off. Their scales and their slime are very important in protecting them from attacks of disease and parasites in the water. It is better to kill a badly damaged fish, or a diseased one, rather than return it to the water where it may spread infection as well as suffering. Always kill fish as quickly as possible.

Leave no litter

Other animals as well can be damaged by careless anglers. Never leave line lying around – particularly fine nylon line, which can at worst kill animals. Water birds may eat lead shot left in the water, and be poisoned by it. Even polythene bags left around can be killers. The best policy is to make sure that you take home absolutely everything that you brought with you – and make sure that you obey the country code.

The future of fishing as a sport depends entirely on how we treat it now so always be thoughtful to the fish and do not be afraid to draw someone else's attention to the fact that they may be being thoughtless!

Take care of the fish and handle them as little as possible. Placing them on a damp sheet before photographing is a good idea; and always return them to the water as soon as you can.

Where to Fish

You cannot just go and fish anywhere you like. First, you may well need a licence. This is issued by the local River Authority, and you need one whether you are fishing a water that is privately owned or one that belongs to a club. A rod licence only allows you to fish with one rod; if you wish to use two or more rods on any fishing outing, you must have the same number of rod licences. You can get your licence at a tackle shop.

Some River Authorities allow people below a certain age to fish without a licence; some allow young people to pay less than the full sum. Check to make sure that you are not paying more than you need to! Remember that if you move from one River Authority's area to another, you will need to buy another licence.

Getting permission

You will need permission to fish on most waters. In coarse fishing this will be from the landowner, or if the water belongs to a club you will be able to buy a ticket which will allow you to fish there for a day or possibly for a season. Most fly-fishing waters are day-ticket waters too, and so you simply buy a permit from the office. This will probably allow you to catch and keep a certain number of fish; if you want to catch more, you will have to take another ticket.

No permits are needed for sea fishing, and you can fish at any time of year.

Close seasons

Fishing all year round would interfere with the fishes' breeding. To prevent this, there is a close season for coarse fish which allows them time to spawn and recover before being caught. For most of England and Wales this is from March 15th to June 15th inclusive, but some parts are different while Scotland and Ireland have no close season. Again, check at your local tackle shop. Trout-fishing seasons depend entirely on the area or the water concerned.

River Authorities

River Authorities will be able to give you information about fishing in your area, and their addresses are listed below. Some of them allow people below a certain age to fish without a licence, and this age is given in brackets. You will not need a licence to fish in Scotland.

River Authorities have by-laws concerning such things as the methods you may use, the taking of fish, and the permitted sizes of net. These are drawn up to make sure that there will be good fishing for everyone, for a long time to come. So it is in your own longterm interests to observe them.

Anglian River Authority, Kingfisher House, Goldhay Way, Orton Goldhay, Peterborough PE2 0ZR (12)
Northumbrian River Authority, Eldon House, Regent Centre, Gosforth, Newcastle upon Tyne NE3 3UD
North West River Authority, Richard Fairclough House, Knutsford Road, Warrington WA14 1HG (14)
Severn/Trent River Authority, Sapphire East, 550 Streetbrook Road, Solihull B91 1QT (14)
Southern River Authority, Guildbourne House, Chatsworth Road, Worthing, West Sussex BN11 1LD
South West River Authority, Manley Ho, Kestrel Way, Exeter EX2 7LQ (10)
Thames River Authority, Kings Meadow House, Kings Meadow Road, Reading RG1 8DG (16)
Welsh/Cymru River Authority, Rivers House/Plas-yr-Afon, St Mellons Business Park, Cardiff CF3 0EG
Wessex River Authority, Rivers House, East Quay, Bridgewater, Somerset TA6 4YS (11)
Yorkshire River Authority, 21 Park Square South, Leeds LS1 2QG (14)

Books to Read

The best way to learn to fish is to go out and practise, but here are some books which you will enjoy reading and which can be very useful.

Sports Starters: Fishing by Gerry Hughes; published by Collins.

Legering by Peter Stone; published by Acro.

The New Encyclopedia of Float Fishing by Billy Lane; published by Pelham Books.

Stillwater Angling by Richard Walker; published by David & Charles.

Geoffrey Bucknall's Book of Fly Fishing; published by Thomas Nelson.

The Young Angler's Handbook by Brian Morland; published by Hamlyn.

Freshwater Fishes of Britain and Europe by Alwyne Wheeler; published by Kingfisher Books.

Societies to Join

There are various societies and associations which help anglers or give them information. Here are some addresses.

Anglers' Co-operative Association, Midland Bank Chambers, 88 Westgate, Grantham, Lincs. NG31 6LT helps anglers fight water pollution.

English Tourist Board, 4 Grosvenor Gardens, London SW1 0DU.

Inland Waterways Association, 114 Regent's Park Road, London NW1 8UQ.

Irish Tourist Board, 150 New Bond Street, London W1Y 0AG.

National Anglers' Council, 11 Cowgate, Peterborough PE1 1LZ was formed to promote and protect the interests of anglers. Clubs and individuals can be members, and it has a free advisory service.

National Federation of Anglers, Halliday House, 2 Wilson Street, Derby aims to protect, promote and improve coarse fishing; it organizes big fishing matches and championships. It has no individual members.

National Federation of Sea Anglers, 26 Downsview Crescent, Uckfield, Sussex TN22 1UB looks after the interests of sea anglers.

Northern Ireland Tourist Board, 11 Berkeley Street, London W1X 6LN.

Salmon and Trout Association, Fishmongers' Hall, London Bridge, London EC4R 9EL works to improve and protect rivers containing trout and salmon.

Scottish Tourist Board, 23 Ravelston Terrace, Edinburgh EH4 3EU.

Sports Council, 16 Upper Woburn Place, London WC1H 0QP.

Welsh Tourist Centre, Glamorgan Street, Brecon.

Many people belong to angling clubs, and your local library should be able to give you a list of those in your neighbourhood. Clubs usually have a junior section for young members, with low membership fees. There are several advantages in belonging to a club. You can fish club water without extra charge, and perhaps buy tackle and bait at special low prices. Many clubs have coaching for young members. And you can join trips to other waters, and take part in fishing matches which the club arranges. Perhaps best of all, you will meet other young anglers.

Glossary

Action (rod) The way in which a rod behaves when casting; for example, a *tip-action* rod concentrates most flexibility in the tip.

AFTM scale The standard for rating the weight of fly-lines and for matching line to rod.

Arlesey bomb A pear-shaped weight used in legering.

Artery forceps Long pincers which are used to remove a hook from a fish's mouth; they should always be used when handling fish such as pike, which can otherwise give you a very nasty bite.

Attractor A fly that does not necessarily imitate any form of life, but which arouses a fish's aggression.

Backing line A long length of line connecting the fly-line to the reel; it comes into use when a fish makes a long run.

Baiting up Introducing bait to an area of water over a period of time before fishing it, thus lulling the fish into a false sense of security.

Bale arm The part of a fixed-spool reel which guides the line on to the reel; it should be opened during casting, but then closed for winding in.

Bird's-nest A tangle of line.

Bite indicator A means of telling that you have a bite when you are legering. The indicator, which can be something like a plastic bottle cap or even a piece of bread, is placed on the line between the first two rings on the rod, and when a fish takes the bait the pull on the line will make the indicator rise towards the rod. More expensive indicators include electronic buzzers and flashing lights for fishing in the dark.

Bob-fly The top dropper in a cast of several flies.

Brandling A small red worm with yellow rings on its body, usually found in manure heaps, which makes a very effective bait.

Bubble float A device used usually together with a monofilament line to provide weight to cast a fly with coarse tackle. It may be filled with water.

Bulge The displacement of the surface of the water by a fish's back when feeding just below the surface; fish feeding in this way are said to be humping.

Caster A maggot in the chrysalis stage, which makes an effective bait.

Casting Using the rod to throw the line, with bait or fly attached, on the water.

Centrepin reel A large-diameter reel that revolves round a central spindle.

Chalk stream A stream or river that is clear because it rises in chalk hills, from springs, and is seldom altered much in level by rainfall.

Check A ratchet or drag that may be used to maintain the tension on a reel to provide resistance to a running fish.

Close season The time of year when fishing is banned, to allow fish to spawn and recover. In most areas of England and Wales the close season for coarse fish is from March 15th to June 15th inclusive, but it varies a little from one area to another. There is no close season in Scotland or Ireland. There are also close seasons for salmon, trout and sea trout.

Coarse fish Any fish that lives in fresh water and is not a member of the salmon family.

Cover a fish To cast a fly so that the fish will see it.

Dapping Allowing a fly to blow in front of you and skip along the surface of the water as the line is taken by the wind.

Disgorger An instrument with which to remove a hook from a fish's mouth.

Drag Situation that occurs when a dry fly skids across the surface instead of floating with the current. Also the brake on a reel.

Drift fishing Fishing from a boat allowed to drift with the wind.

Drogue An underwater parachute-type of device attached to a boat to slow the drift or hold it in a certain position as it drifts.

Dry fly An artificial fly that floats on the water surface.

False-casting The process of lengthening the line in the air by back and forward casts until enough line is in the air to make the final cast.

Fast-recovery reel Another term for MULTIPLIER REEL.

Ferrule The joint which is used to connect rod sections.

Figure-eighting A method of bunching the line in the palm of the hand when retrieving in fly fishing.

Fixed-spool reel This is the most popular type of reel in coarse fishing today. The spool does not move while the line is wound in or let out over its lip.

Flash The reflecting of light by a fly due to the inclusion of tinsel in the dressing.

Floatant A substance used to make lines float, also applied to dry flies to ensure their long-floating qualities.

Floater or floating fly Other terms for a dry fly.

Fly-line the weighted line used in flyfishing.

Freelining A way of coarse fishing, used often for carp and chub, in which a bait is attached to the line and fished without a float or weights attached. This attempts to allow the bait to fish as naturally as if it was unattached to a line.

Fry The young of any fish.

Gaff An instrument, consisting of a metal hook attached to a stout pole, used for landing heavy fish.

Game fish Of freshwater fish, a term used for members of the salmon family; in salt water, generally any fish of fine sporting ability.

Groundbait Bait, not usually that on the hook, which is scattered to keep the fish feeding in a particular area.

Hackle The feather tied on a fly immediately behind the eye of the hook.

Hatch A large quantity of flies coming off the water; also, a series of boards placed across a stream to regulate the flow.

Imitator A fly that represents a form of food that a fish may be feeding on.

Landing net A net on a pole in which the played-out fish is brought ashore.

Larva The underwater stage of some forms of insect.

Lateral line The line of cells along a fish's flank through which it senses vibrations and movement in the water.

Laying on A type of float fishing in which the last one or two shot and the bait lie on the bottom.

Leader The length of nylon connecting the fly-line to the fly.

Legering Fishing with the bait kept on the bottom by a weight, and without a float.

Lie The resting place of a fish, or what it may consider to be its territory.

Limit The maximum number or weight of fish the rules of the water permit to be killed.

Lobworm The large type of earthworm commonly found in gardens.

Lure A term used to describe all artificial bait; in trout fishing, a large wet fly.

Minnow A small fish found almost everywhere in fresh water, which is an important item in the diet of most fish.

Monofilament Ordinary single-strand nylon fishing line.

Multiplier reel A reel geared to revolve the drum more than once for each turn of the handle.

Nymph Angler's term for the stage in the life-cycle of some water-bred insects, after the egg and before the winged stage; imitation fly of this stage.

Paternoster A tackle rig with one or more hooks and a large lead at the bottom, with the hooks on nylon droppers or on wire or plastic arms. This keeps the baits from entangling the main line and is useful in sea fishing and in coarse fishing.

Playing a fish 'Fighting' the fish after hooking it to tire it so that it may be landed.

Point The slim tip of a leader, also called a tippet.

Point fly The fly fished at the farthest point of the leader on a team; also known as the tail fly.

Priest A weighted club used to kill a landed fish with a blow to the back of the head.

Putting down a fish Causing a fish to stop feeding, usually by fishing clumsily and scaring it into inactivity or into bolting.

Recovering Pulling back the line by hand or by winding the reel.

Resting a fish Leaving a fish after it has been 'put down' in the hope that it will begin feeding again later.

Retrieving Fishing a fly back towards you by recovering the line.

Rings The guides along a rod through which the line passes.

Rise The action of a fish coming up to take a fly from the water's surface; collectively, a period when fish are feeding greedily on the surface.

Shooting-head Fly-line which tapers to its narrowest at the front; about half the length of an ordinary fly-line, it is joined to a length of lighter backing and used for casting longer distances.

Spate A flood or an increase in the water flowing in a river.

Specimen fish A fish that is of exceptional weight for a particular water and in good condition.

Spinner The final stage in the life-cycle of upwing flies; known, after mating, as 'spent spinners'.

Striking Setting the hook into a fish that has taken the fly by raising the rod.

'Sulking' Term used of a hooked fish that takes to the bottom or hides behind a snag and refuses to budge.

Sunken fly Another term for WET FLY.

Swim A term used by coarse-fishermen to describe a place where fishing is usually good.

Tail fly Another term for POINT FLY.

Tandem hook Two (or more) hooks tied one behind the other.

Team of flies A number of flies, usually three or four, fished on the same leader.

Treble hook A hook that has three bends and barbs brazed together to give all-round hooking capacity.

Trolling Trailing the line behind a moving boat.

Trotting A type of float fishing in which both float and tackle are taken downstream by the current.

Weight-forward taper A line that has its weight concentrated in the forward section, used for casting longer distances.

Wet fly An artificial fly fished beneath the surface.

Index

Entries in *italics* indicate pictures

A

Arlesey bomb *46*, 112
Artery forceps 49, 112
Attractor 82, 112
Automatic reel *66*
Avington, Hampshire *77*

B

Backing line 112
Bait 11, 14, 22, 30–33, *30–33*, 45, 98–99, *98–99*
  bread 14, 15, 18, 19, 30, 45, 93
  cheese 20, *33*, *41*
  crabs 92, 93, 94, 95, 98, *99*, 100, 104
  crayfish 32
  deadbait 14, 21, 23, 32, 45, 47
  floating crusts 16, 18
  groundbait *32*, 33, 113
  hemp 30
  insects 32
  lugworms 92, 93, 94, 98, *99*
  maggots 13, 14, 15, 18, 19, 20, 21, 22, 30, *30*, 45
  meat 32, *41*
  particle bait 32
  pet food 18
  ragworms 93, 94, 95, 98, *98*, 104
  sand eel 92, 93, 98, *98*, 104
  shellfish 93, 95, 99, 100, 104
  slugs 32
  sprats 95, 99
  squid 93, 98
  sweetcorn 18, 20, 31, 45
  wheat 32
  worms 13, 14, 15, 18, 19, 20, 21, 22, 30, *30*, 45
Bale arm 50, 112
Bank fishing 86
Bank stick 37
Barb 28, *28*
Barbel 19–20, *20*, *21*, 24, 25, 28, 30, *40*
Barrel lead *46*
Bass 92, *92*, *95*, 98, 104, 105
Beach caster 96
Beach fishing *9*, 91, 92, 93, 95, 109

Bite indicator 47, *47*, 112
Bleak 22
Blood knot *67*
Blow lines 81
Blue-winged olive spinner 57
Boat fishing 77, 86, *86*, *90*, 90–91, 91, 92, 93, 94, 95, 96, *97*, 108, 109
Boat rod 96, *97*
Bobbin indicator 47, *47*
Bob fly 83, 112
Breaking strain 27
Bream 17, 18–19, *31*, 89, *89*, 91, 94, 95, 107
  silver bream 19, *19*
Brook rod 65
Bubble float 112
Bullet lead *46*

C

Canals *21*, 106
Cane rod 64, *65*
Carbon fibre
  reel *66*
  rod 64, *65*, 96
Carp *8*, 17–18, *17*, *18*, 24, 45, 47
  crucian carp 18, *19*
Cast *see* Leader
Caster 112
Casting *9*, 112
  coarse fishing 50–51, *50–51*
  fly fishing 58, 70–72, *70–72*, 80, 85
  sea fishing 102–103, *102–103*
Centrepin reel 26, *26*, 51, 112
Chalk stream *73*, 112
Check 112
Chub *10*, *11*, 16, *16*, 25, 28, *33*, *40*, *41*, 42, 43, 48, 89, 107
Close season 112
Clothing 34–35, *34–35*
Clubs 55, 111
Coarse fish 12–23, *12–23*
Coarse fishing *8*, *9*, 10–53, *10–53*, 89, *89*, 112
Cod 91, 93, 98, 99, *103*
Coffin lead *46*
Competitive fishing 27, 106–107, *106–107*
Conger eel *93*, 94, *94*, 98, 99
Conservation 83, 109
Country code 108, 109

D

Dab 91
Dace 19, *19*
Daddy-long-legs 68, *80*
Dapping *81*, 112
Deadbait 14, 21, 22, 32, 45, 47
Disgorger 22, 112
Dogfish 91, 93
Double-taper line 65, *65*
Drag 112
Drift fishing *86*, 112
Drogue 112
Drop net 97, 100, 105
Dry flies *68*, 81
Dry fly fishing 78, 79, 80–81, *80–81*, 86

E

Eddies *40*, 42
Eel 12, 21, *21*, 28, 32, 47

F

Fast-recovery reel 112
Ferrule 38, 112
Fish
  anatomy *12*
  coarse 12–23, *12–23*
  hybrid 23, *23*, 61
  sea 92–95, *92–95*
  trout and salmon 57–88, *57–88*
Fisheries 55, 60, 77
Fish farming 55, 61
Fishing matches 27, 106–107, *106–107*
Fixed-spool reel 26, 27, 50, 51, 96, 112
Flatfish 92, *92*, 101
Float 29, *29*, *38*, 39, *44*, 44–45, *45*, 96, 97
Floatant 81, 112
Float fishing
  coarse 40, 44–45, *44–45*
  sea 92, 100, 101, 103, 104
Float-fishing rod 25
Floating line *64*, 65, 78, 79, 82, 84, 85
Flounder 92, *92*
Fly 55, 68–69, *68–69*
  dry flies 80, *80*, 87, 89, 112
  salmon flies 63
  wet flies 82, *82*, 83, 113
  see also Nymph *and* Lure

Fly casting 70–72. *70–72*
Fly fishing 9, *9*. 54–89, *54–89*, 109
Free-lining 17, 112

G
Gaff 105, 113
Garfish *92*, 94
Glass fibre
    rod 24, 64, *65*, 96
    spigot 38
Gravel pit *see* Reservoir
Grayling 57, *60*, 61, *61*, 62, *73*
Grey mullet 93, *93*, 101
Groundbait *32*, 33, 113
Gudgeon 22, *23*

H
Hackle *68*, *80*, 113
Half-blood knot *67*
Handling fish *11*, *13*, 14, 15, 21,
    53, 73, *75*, 94, 109, *109*
Harbour fishing 91, *91*, 92, 93, 94,
    100–101, *100–101*
Harness *97*
Hatch 113
Herring 32, 94, 95, 99
Hooks 11, 28, *28*, 39, 45, 67, *67*,
    75, *75*, 97, *98*, 101
Hybrids 23, *23*

I
Imitator 82, 113

K
Kempton reservoir *87*
Knots *39*, 67, *67*

L
Lakes 58, 59, 76, 79
Landing
    coarse fishing 29, *29*, 43,
       52, 52–53
    fly fishing *62*, 63, *66*, *74*, 74–75
    rock fishing 104–105
Leader 55, 80, 82, 83, 85, 88, 113
Leads *96*, 97, 101, 102
Legering 40, *41*, 46–47, *46–47*,
    104, 113
Leger rods 25
Licences 110
Lily pads *8*, 43
Line 26, 27, 55, *64*, 65, *81*, 107,
    109
Loach 22, *23*
Lobworm 45, 113,
Loose feeding 33
Lure 113
    coarse fishing 25, *48*, 48–49,
       89, *89*
    fly fishing 68, *68*, 87–88, *88*

M
Mackerel 32, 90, *90*, 92, *92*, 94,
    95, *99*, 104
Maggots 13, 14, 15, 18, 19, 20, 21,
    22, 30, *30*, 45
Match fishing 8, *27*, 106–107,
    106–107
Mayfly *81*, 84
Minnow 21, 33, 113
Monofilament 113
Mullet 91
Multiplier reel 27, 51, *66*, 96, 103,
    113

N
Needle knot *67*
Net 52, *52*, 53, *53*, *66*, 73–75,
    73–75, *96*, 97
Night fishing *59*, 82
Nymph 68, *69*, 84, *84*, 85, 86, 89,
    113
Nymphing 78, 84–85, *84–85*, 86

P
Particle bait 32
Paternoster 97, 113
Paternostering 100, 101, *101*, 104
Peg 106
Perch 12, *13*, 32, 42, 43, 48, 89
Permits 110
Pike *8*, *11*, 12, 13, 14, *14*, 15, 24,
    25, 28, 29, 42, *42*, 43, 44, 48,
    49, 89, *89*
Pike bung *44*
Pike-perch *see* Zander
Pilot float *44*
Pirk 99
Plaice 91, 94
Playing a fish 52, *62*, 73, *73*, 113
Plug 28, 48, *48*, 49
Point 113
Pollack 93, 104
Pope *see* Ruffe
Porbeagle 95
Pouting 95
Priest *64*, 113

Q
Quill float 29, 44

R
Ray 94
    sting ray *93*, 94
Reel
    coarse fishing 26, *26*, 26–27, *27*, 39
    fly fishing 66, *66*
    sea fishing 96
Regulations 110
Reservoirs *9*, 42, *43*, 59, 60, 77,
    77, 79, 86, 87, *87*

Rig 90
Rings 25, *25*, 29, 39, *44*, 113
River Authorities 110
Rivers 10, 16, 20, 42–43, *42–43*,
    58, 76, 77, 106, *106*
Roach *8*, 12, *12*, *13*, 16, *17*, 25, 31,
    31, 32, *33*, 42, 43, 45, 89
    roach-bream 23, *23*
Roach pole 27
Roll casting 72
Rock fishing *90*, 92, 93, 104–105,
    104–105, 109
Rod
    assembly 27, *38*, 39
    coarse fishing 11, 24–25, *25*
    continental style 27, 107
    fly fishing 64–65, *64–65*
    maintenance 38, *66*
    sea fishing 91, 96, *96*, 97
Rod rest 46, 47, *47*
Rudd *8*, *16*, 16–17, *17*
Ruffe 22, 23

S
Safety 40, 53, *74*, 83, *83*, 91, 94,
    95, 102, 104, 108–109
Salmon 9, 57, 59, 62–63, *62–63*
Sea fishing 9, *9*, 90–105, *90–105*
Shade 10, *41*, 43, *79*
Shark 95, 99
Shooting head 65, *65*, *67*, 113
Short-lining *86*
Shot, shotting 28, 29, *38*, 39, 44
Silver bream 19, *19*
Single-action reel *66*
Sinking line *64*, 65, 78, 79, 82, 84,
    88
Sliding float 29, 97, 101
Smolt *63*
Snap tackle *28*
Societies 111
Specimen fish 113
Spinner 14, *48*, 49, 89, 92, 94, *97*,
    99, 101, 104, 113
Spinning 48–49, *48–49*, 92, 104
Spinning rod 25
Spoon *see* Spinner
Sprat 32, 49
Stillwater fishing *85*, 86–88, *86–88*
Stocking fish 55, *55*, 58, 60, 76, 77
Stream, trout 58, *61*, *63*, 76, *76*,
    78–79, *79*
Strike 81, *84*, 85
Swimfeeder 25, *33*
Swing tip indicator 47, *47*

T
Tackle 11
    coarse fishing 24–29, *24–29*,
       36–39, *36–39*

fly fishing 64–67, *64–67*
  sea fishing 91, 96–97, *96–97*
Tackle box *36*, 37, *37*
Tailer *62*
Tail fly 113
Tandem hook 113
Tench 8, 12, 15, *15*, 17
Tope 94, *95*, 99
Treble hook 28, *28*, 113
Troll, trolling 92, 113
Trotting 115
Trout 9, *54*, 55, 56–62, *56–62, 70*,
    73, 74, *74*, 75, 109
  brook 57, 61, *61*
  brown 56, *56*, 57–59, *60*, 74
  rainbow 9, *9*, 56, *56*, 57, *60*,
    60–61, 74
  sea 59, *59*, 61, 82

Turbot 95
Turle knot *67*
Tying flies 68–69, *68–69*

U
Umbrella 37, *37*

W
Wading 83, *83*
Waggler float 45
Wake 83, 85
Waters
  coarse fishing 40–43, *40–43*
  fly fishing 76–77, *76–77*, 86–88,
    86–88
  sea fishing 90–91, *90–91*,
    100–101, *100–101*, 104–105,

    104–105
Weather 40, 41, 43, 78, 88
Weight-forward line 65, *65*, 113
Weights *33*, 46, *46*, 101
  see also Leads *and* Legering
Wet fly fishing 78, 79, 82–83,
  82–83, 113
Whiting 95
Windbeater float 45
Wire trace *28*, 94
Worms 13, 14, 15, 18, 19, 20, 21,
  22, 30, *30*, 45, 98, *98*, 99, *99*
Wrasse *90*, 94, 104

Z
Zander 22, *22*, 28, 48, 49, 89, *89*
Zoomer float 45

ACKNOWLEDGEMENTS

Cover: Mike Millman; 6 left Angling Photo Service, right Mike Millman; 7 left Mike Millman, right Brian Furzer; 8 Mike Millman; 9 top Angling Photo Service, bottom Brian Furzer; 10 top and bottom Bob Church; 11 top Angling Photo Service, bottom Peter Stone; 12 Peter Stone; 13 & 14 Bob Church, 15 Peter Stone, 16 & 17 Bob Church; 18 top Angling Photo Service, bottom Bob Church; 20 Angling Photo Service; 21 Bob Church; 22 Bob Church; 23 Angling Photo Service; 24 Mike Millman; 25 top right Angling Photo Service, bottom right Brian Furzer; 26 Brian Furzer; 27 top right Brian Furzer, bottom left Angling Photo Service; 28 top and centre Brian Furzer, bottom Mike Millman; 29 top left Brian Furzer, bottom left Peter Stone; 30 top Mike Millman, bottom Brian Furzer; 31 top Brian Furzer, bottom Angling Photo Service; 32 Mike Millman; 33 top Mike Millman, bottom Brian Furzer; 34 Bob Church; 35 top Bob Church, bottom Brian Furzer; 36 top Peter Stone, bottom Brian Furzer; 37 Mike Millman; 38 Brian Furzer; 40 top Peter Stone, bottom Brian Furzer; 41 Peter Stone; 42 Bob Church; 43 Bob Church; 44 Angling Photo Service; 45 Brian Furzer; 46 Brian Furzer; 47 Brian Furzer; 48 top Angling Photo Service, bottom Brian Furzer; 39 top Bob Church, bottom Brian Furzer; 50 Brian Furzer; 51 Brian Furzer; 52 top and bottom Bob Church; 53 Bob Church; 54 G. L. Carlisle; 55 Arthur Oglesby; 56 Brian Furzer; 57 top Bernard Cecil Hall, centre Taff Price, bottom G.L. Carlisle; 58 Arthur Oglesby, 59 top and centre Arthur Oglesby, bottom N. Nevison; 60 left above Peter Stone, below N. Cranfield, right Bob Church; 61 G.L. Carlisle; 62 left Nick Cranfield, right British Columbia Tourist Office; 63 top Nick Cranfield, centre Arthur Oglesby; 64 top and bottom Brian Furzer; 65 top and bottom Brian Furzer; 66 top left Brian Furzer, right Mike Millman, centre and bottom Natural Science Photos; 67 Arthur Oglesby; 68 top Brian Furzer, bottom left Natural Science Photos, right Brian Furzer; 69 bottom left Arthur Oglesby, right Brian Furzer; 70 top Brian Furzer, bottom Arthur Oglesby; 72 top Brian Furzer, bottom Arthur Oglesby; 73 top N. Cranfield, bottom Brian Furzer; 74 N. Cranfield, bottom Peter Stone; 75 left from top Peter Stone, Arthur Oglesby, N. Cranfield, right Bob Church; 76 G.L. Carlisle; 77 Brian Furzer, bottom Angling Photo Service; 78 Brian Furzer; 80 Roy Shaw; 81 G. L. Carlisle; 83 top Brian Furzer, bottom Nick Cranfield; 84 left T. Pierce, right Natural Science Photos; 85 N. Cranfield; 86 Arthur Oglesby; 87 Angling Photo Service; 88 top Brian Furzer, bottom N. Nevison; 89 top and centre Bob Church, bottom Brian Furzer; 90 top Mike Millman, bottom Angling Photo Service; 91 top Trevor Housby, bottom Angling Photo Service; 92 Angling Photo Service; 93 Trevor Housby; 94 Trevor Housby; 95 top Bob Church, bottom Angling Photo Service; 96 top Mike Millman, bottom Trevor Housby; 97 top Angling Photo Service, bottom Mike Millman; 97 top and bottom Angling Photo Service; 99 top left Trevor Housby, bottom left Angling Photo Service, bottom right Mike Millman; 100 top and bottom Mike Millman; 101 top Angling Photo Service; 102 Mike Millman; 103 centre left and bottom right Angling Photo Service; 104 Trevor Housby; 105 Mike Millman; 106 Angling Photo Service; 107 top Brian Furzer, bottom Angling Photo Service; 108 Angling Photo Service; 109 Bob Church.